RECORDED VERSIONS GUITAR

AUTHENTIC TRANSCRIPTIONS
WITH NOTES AND TABLATURE

**Transcribed by
JEFF CATANIA
and
HEMME LUTTJEBOER**

from the cradle - eric clapton

ISBN 0-7935-4030-5

This publication is not for sale in
the E.C. and/or Australia
or New Zealand.

HAL•LEONARD CORPORATION

777 W. BLUEMOUND RD. P.O. BOX 13819 MILWAUKEE, WI 53213

Blues Before Sunrise

Words and Music by Leroy Carr

MCA music publishing

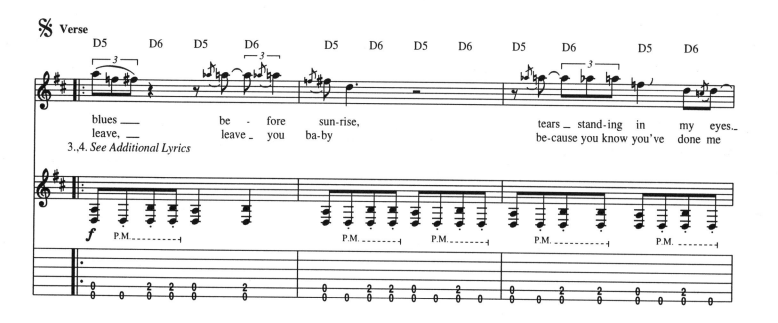

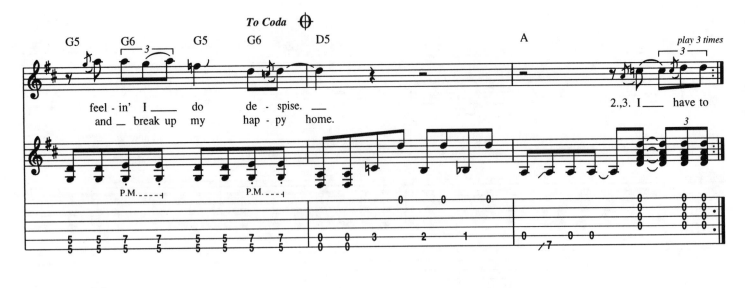

feel - in' I ___ do de - spise. ___

and ___ break up my hap - py home.

2.,3. I ___ have to

Guitar Solo

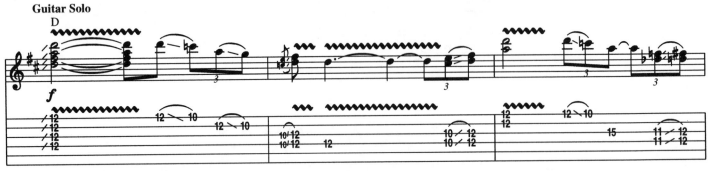

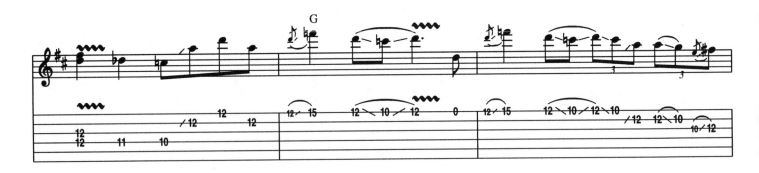

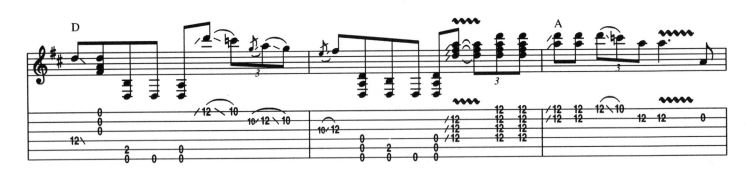

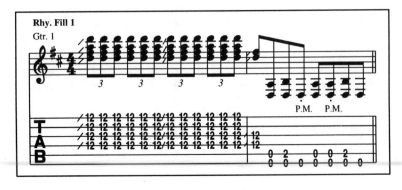

Rhy. Fill 1

Gtr. 1

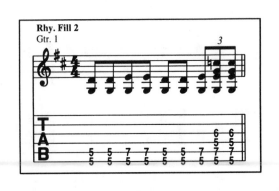

Rhy. Fill 2

Gtr. 1

D.S. al Coda

4. Well, now

Coda

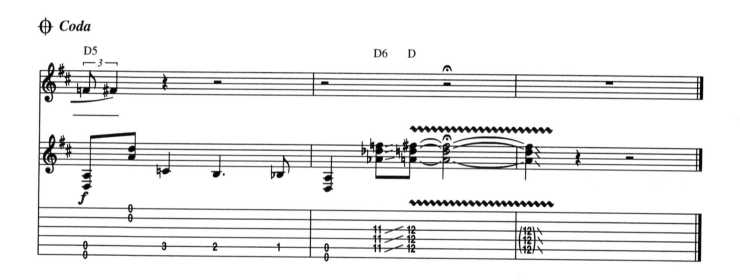

Additional Lyrics

3. I have to leave,
   Leave you baby.
   I'm gonna leave you all alone.
   I'm gonna leave you baby,
   I'm gonna leave you all alone.
   I'm gonna pack up and leave you darlin',
   Because you know you've done me wrong.

4. Goodbye, goodbye baby.
   I'll see you on some rainy day.
   Well, now goodbye baby.
   I'll see you on some rainy day.
   You can go ahead now little darlin',
   'Cause I want you to have your way.

Third Degree

Written by Willie Dixon and Eddie Boyd

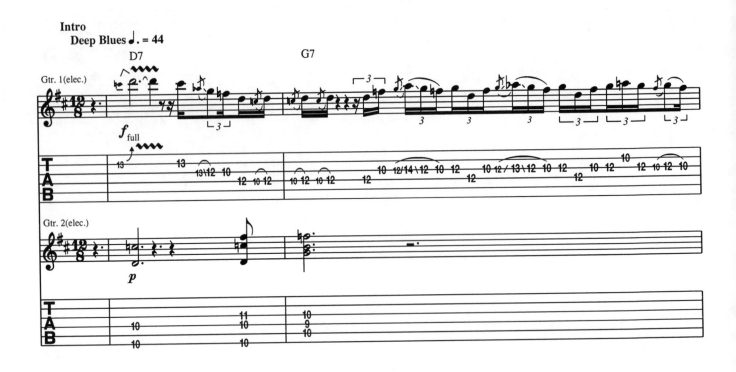

I _ can't see a thing. _ You got me 'cused of pet-tin' _ and I can't e - ven _ raise my hand. _

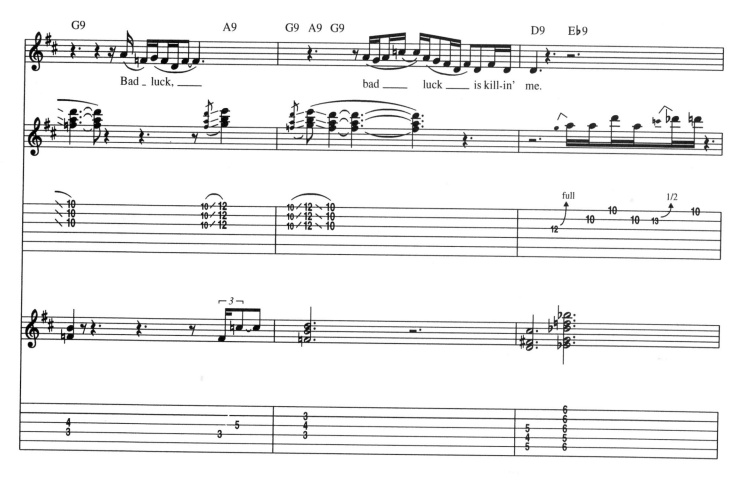

Bad _ luck, _ bad _ luck _ is kill-in' me.

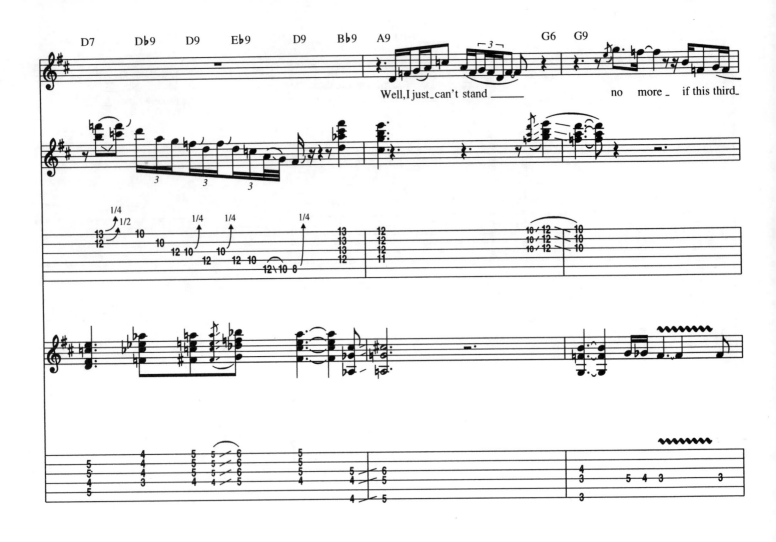

Well, I just_can't stand _____ no more _ if this third_

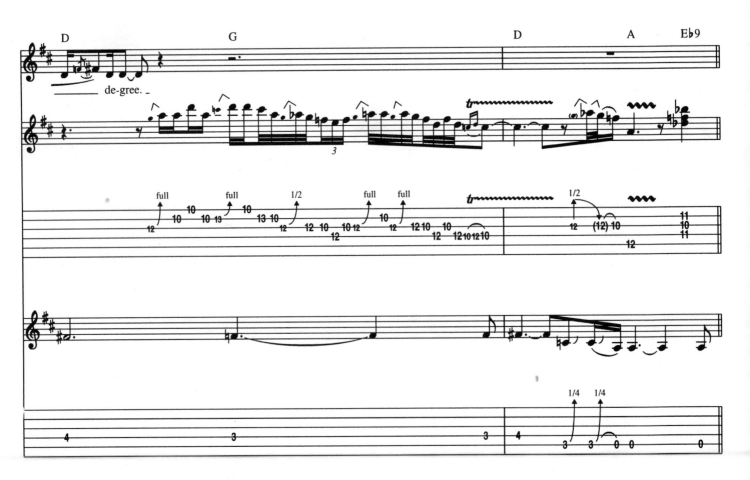

de-gree.

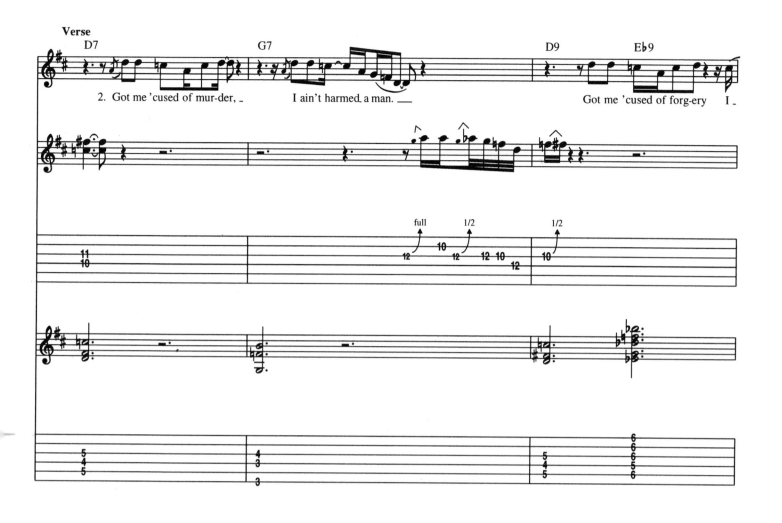

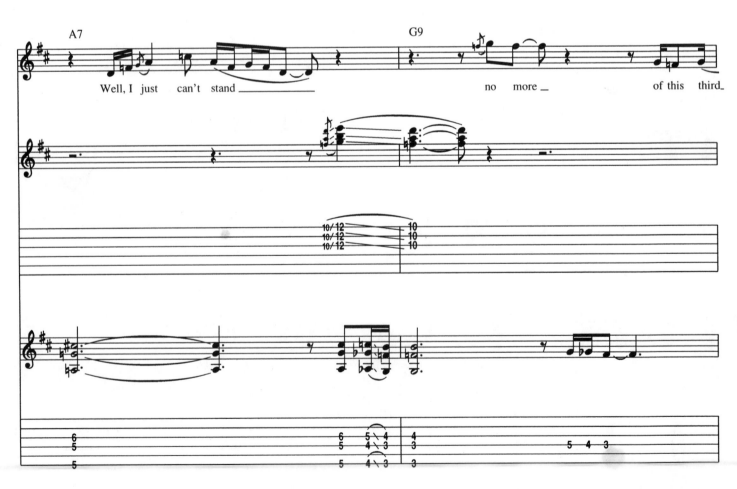

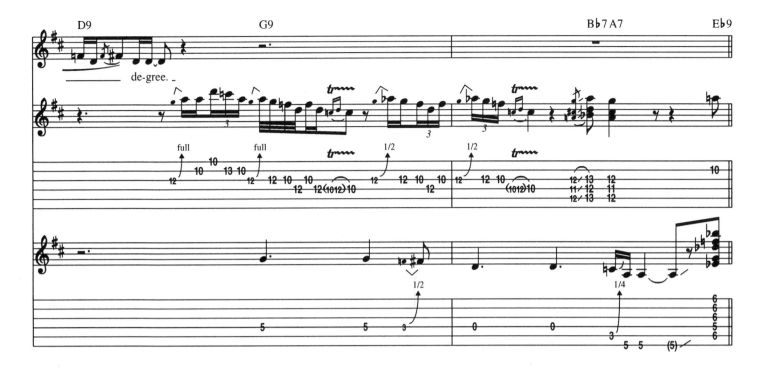

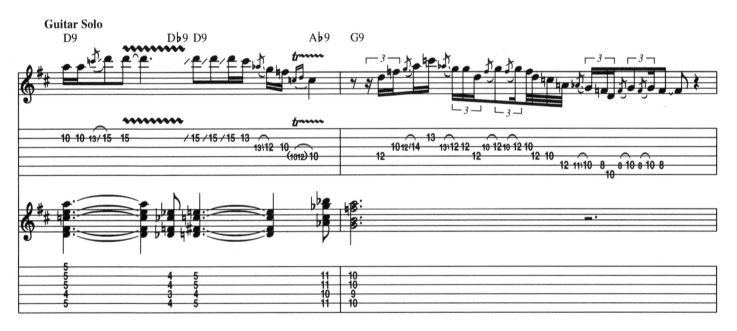

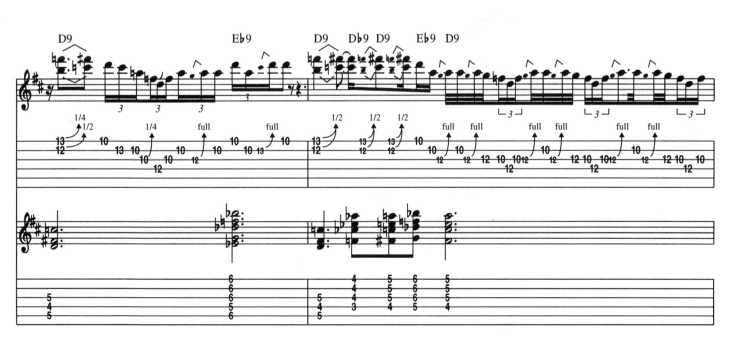

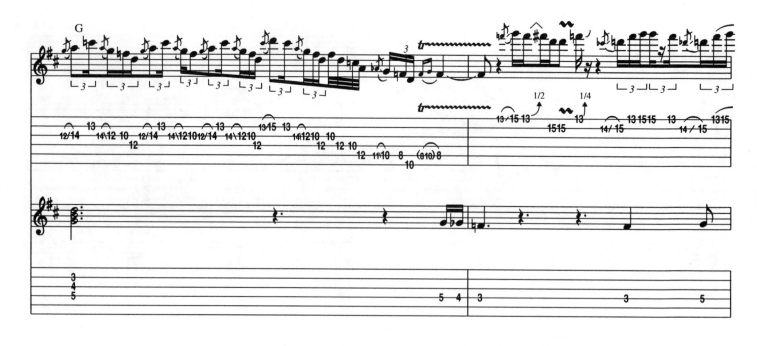

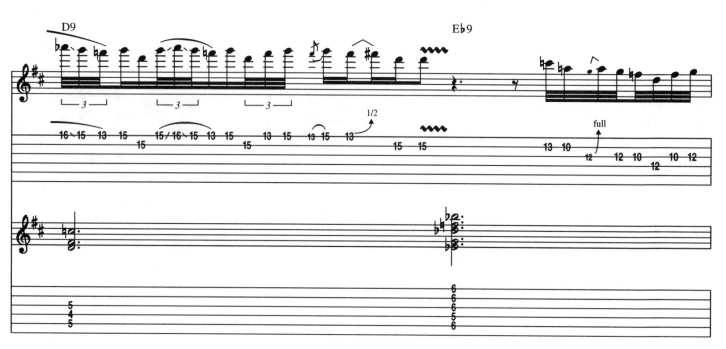

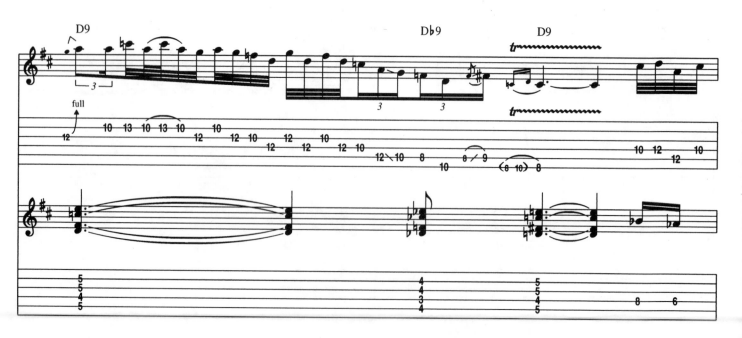

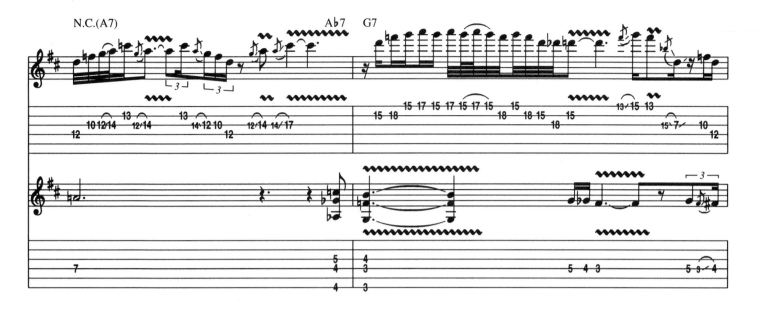

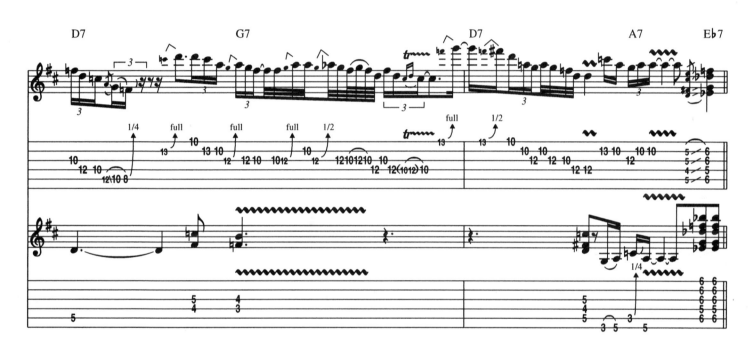

Verse

3. Got me 'cused of tax-es, ___ I ain't got a dime. ___ Got me 'cused of chil-dren

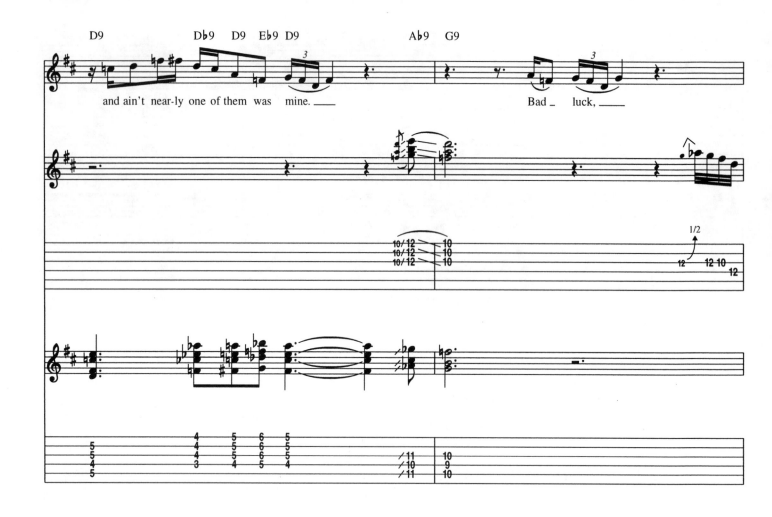

and ain't near-ly one of them was mine. ___ Bad _ luck, ___

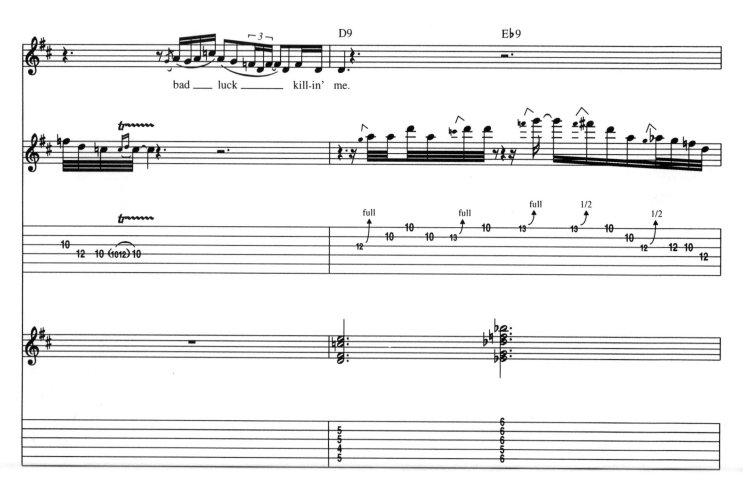

bad ___ luck _____ kill-in' me.

Well, I just can't stand _____

no more of this third _____ de-gree.

Reconsider Baby

Words and Music by Lowell Fulson

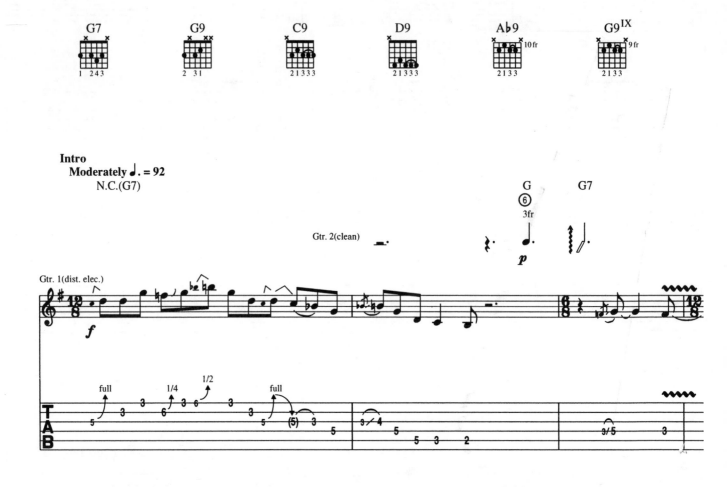

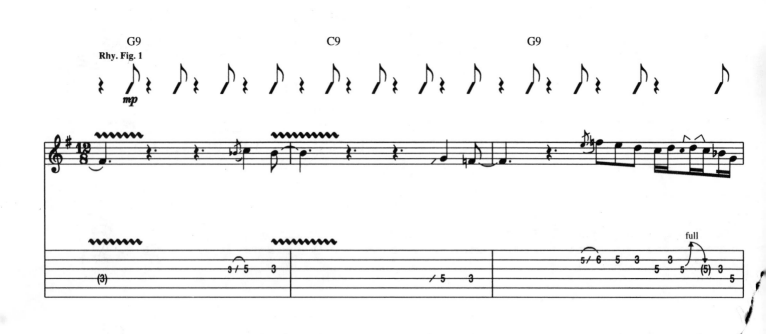

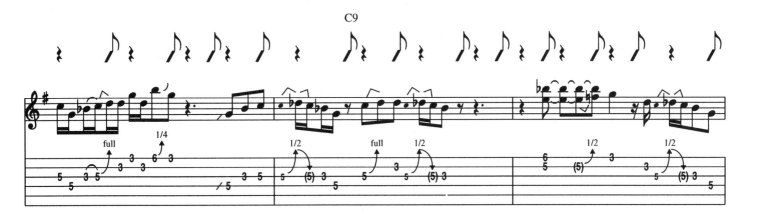

End Rhy. Fig. 1

1. So ____

Verse

Gtr. 2: w/ Rhy. Fig. 1

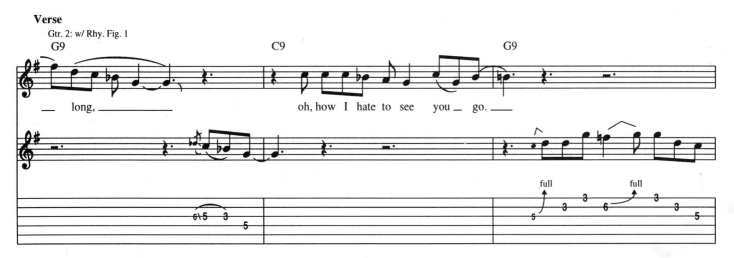

long, ____ oh, how I hate to see you __ go. __

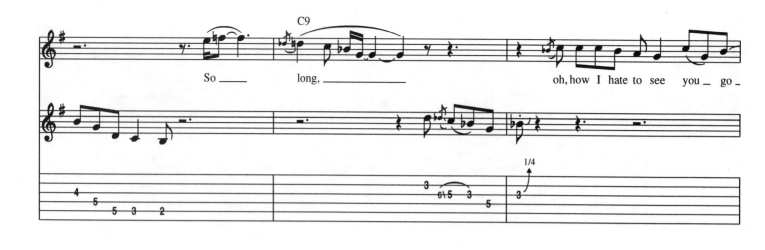

So ____ long, _____ oh, how I hate to see you ___ go ___

and ___ the way that I ___ will miss you.

I ___ guess ___ you would nev-er know. ___

2. We've been to-geth -

Verse

Gtr. 2: w/ Rhy. Fig. 1

- er so ___ long ___ to have to sep-a-rate this way. _____

3. You __ said you

Verse

I'm Your Hoochie Coochie Man

Written by Willie Dixon

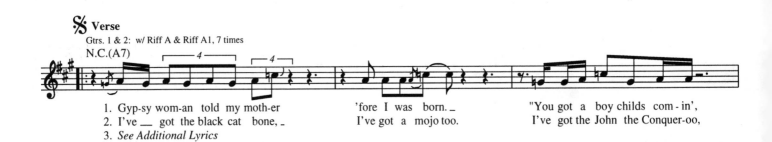

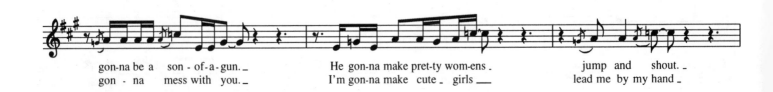

1. Gyp-sy wom-an told my moth-er 'fore I was born. "You got a boy childs com-in',
2. I've got the black cat bone, I've got a mojo too. I've got the John the Conquer-oo,
3. *See Additional Lyrics*

gon-na be a son- of-a-gun. He gon-na make pret-ty wom-ens jump and shout.
gon - na mess with you. I'm gon-na make cute girls lead me by my hand

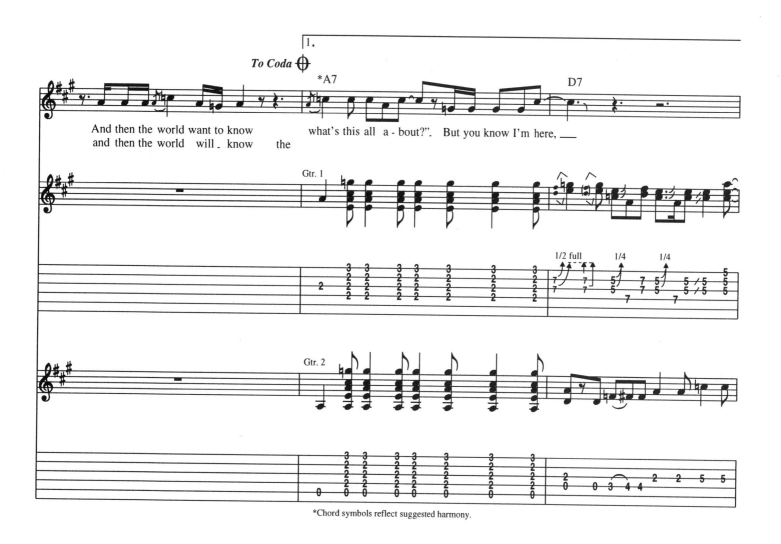

*Chord symbols reflect suggested harmony.

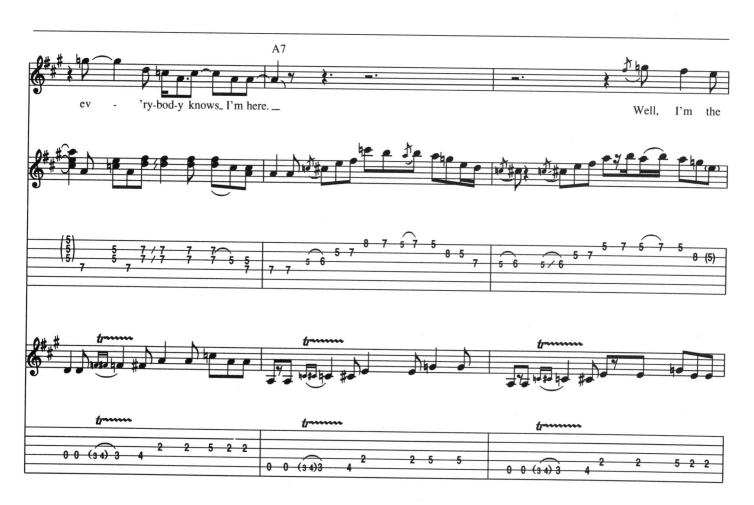

Hoo - chie Coo-chie man,   ev - - 'ry-bod-y knows I'm here. ____

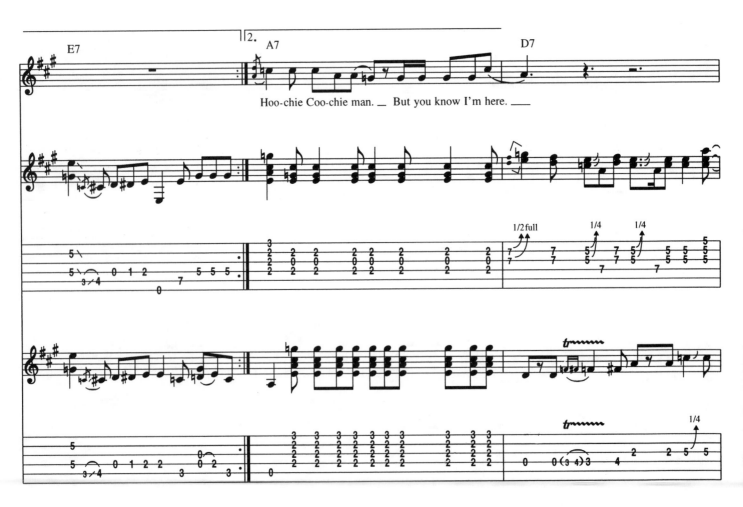

Hoo-chie Coo-chie man. ___ But you know I'm here. ____

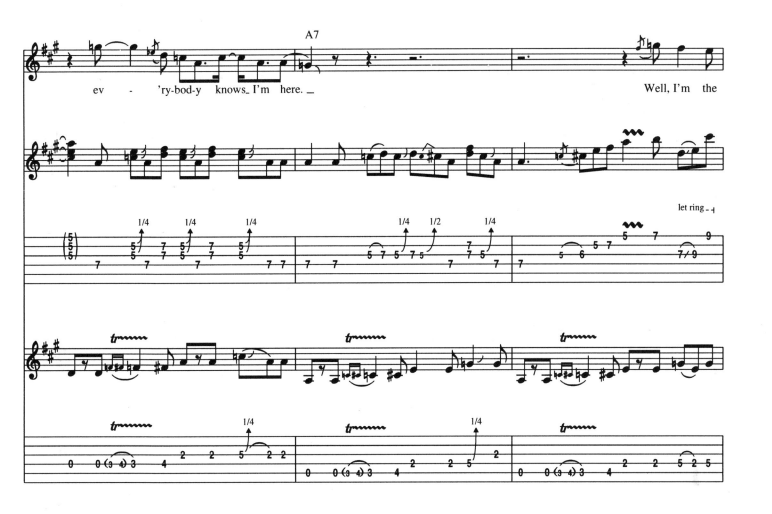

ev - 'ry-bod-y knows_ I'm here. _

Well, I'm the

Hoo - chie Coo-chie man, _

ev - 'ry-bod-y knows I'm here. _____

Harmonica Solo

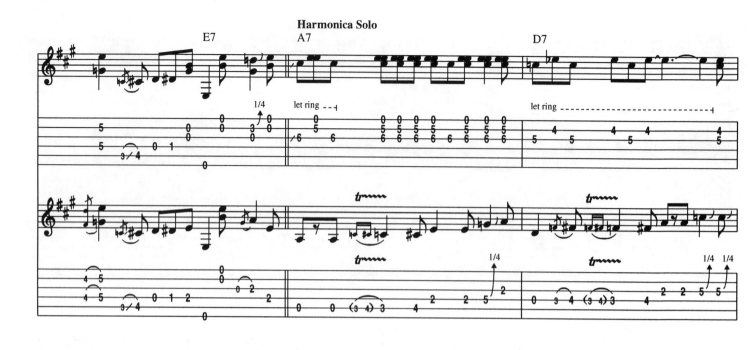

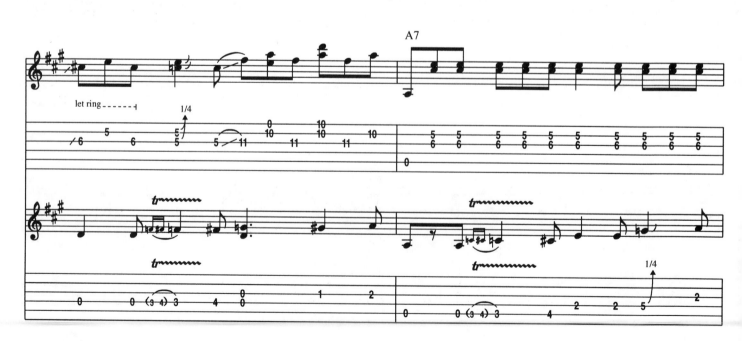

26

D.S. al Coda

Coda

don't you mess with me — 'cause you know I'm here, —   ev - 'ry-bod-y knows I'm here..

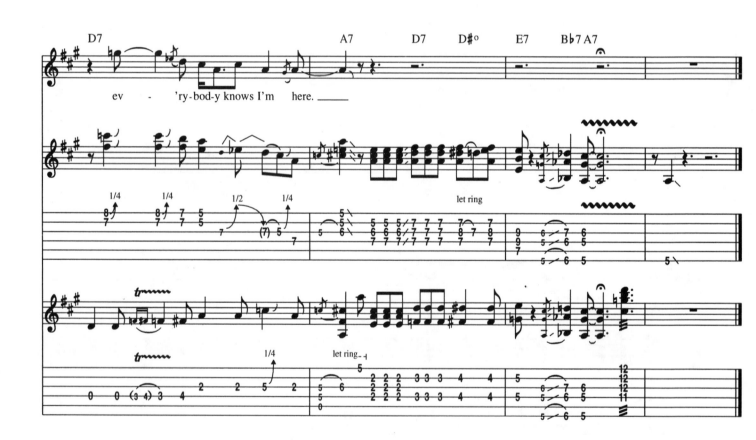

Additional Lyrics

3. On the seventh hour, on the seventh day,
   On the seventh month, the seventh doctor say,
   "You were born for good luck, that you'll see."
   I got seven hundred dollars.
   Don't you mess with me, 'cause you know I'm here.

Five Long Years

Words and Music by Eddie Boyd

*Chord symbols reflect suggested tonality.

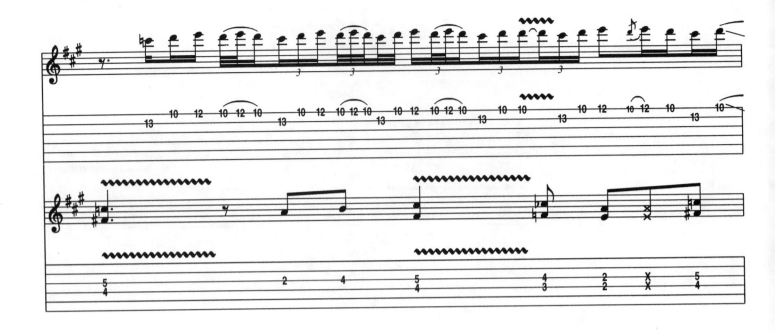

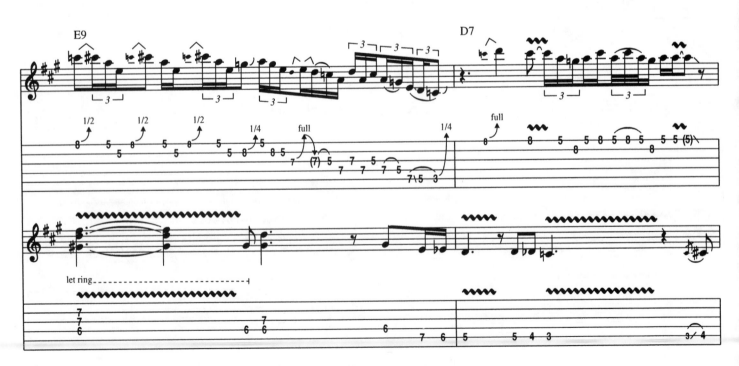

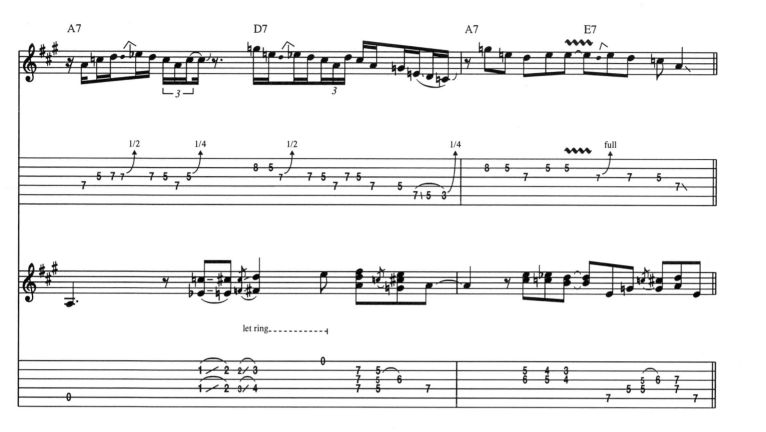

Verse

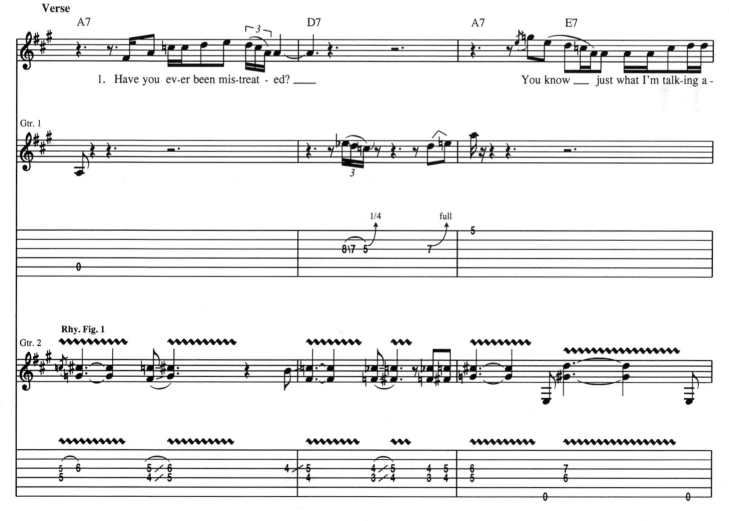

1. Have you ev-er been mis-treat - ed? ____   You know ____ just what I'm talk-ing a -

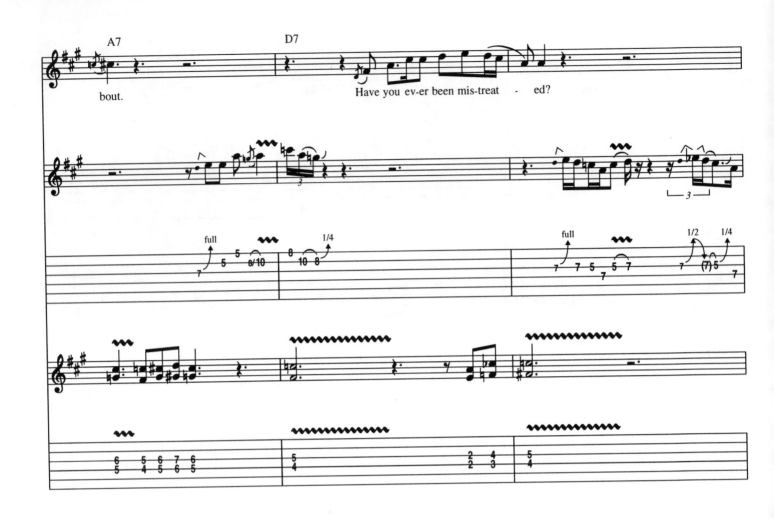

bout.

Have you ev-er been mis-treat - ed?

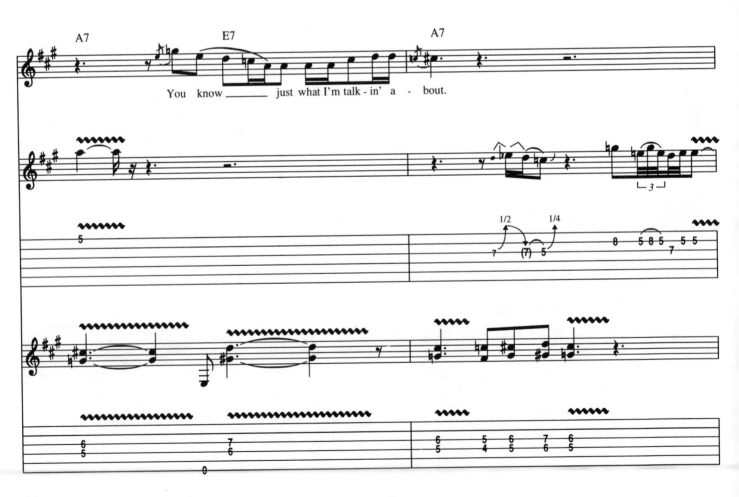

You know _____ just what I'm talk - in' a - bout.

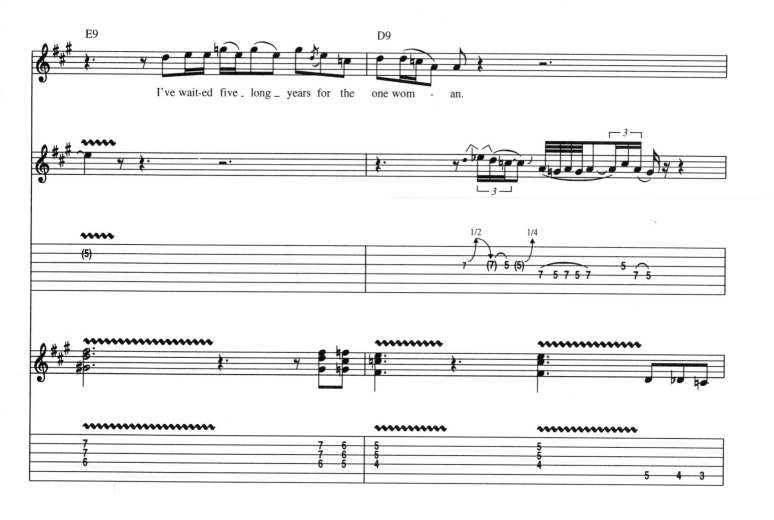

I've wait-ed five _ long _ years for the   one wom - an.

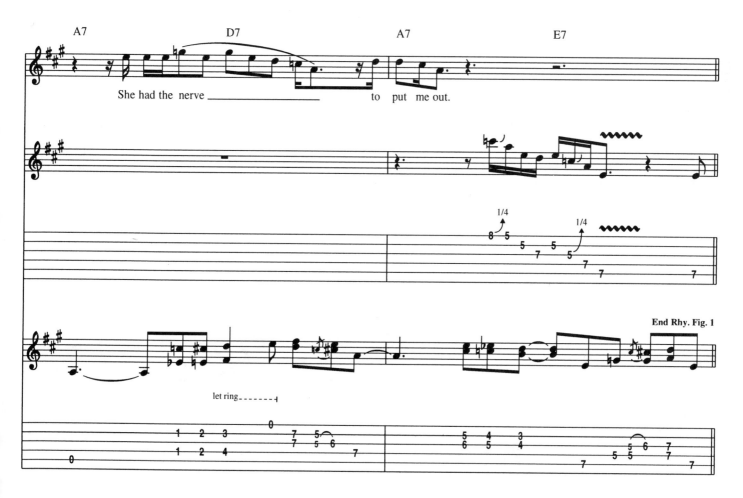

She had the nerve _____   to put me out.

End Rhy. Fig. 1

let ring_____

Gtr. 2: w/ Rhy. Fill 1

I've wait-ed five long years for one wom - an.

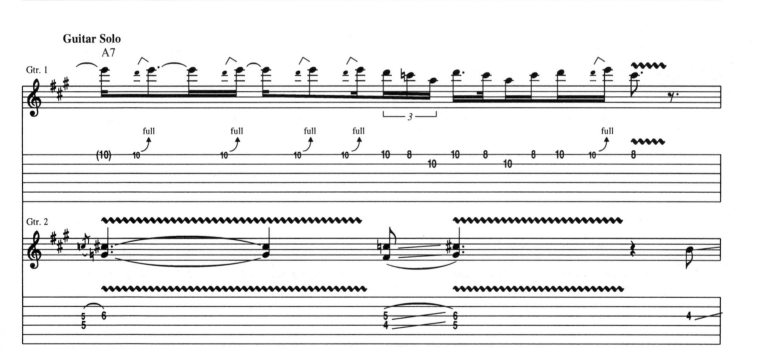

She had the nerve _____ to put me out.

Guitar Solo

Rhy. Fill 1

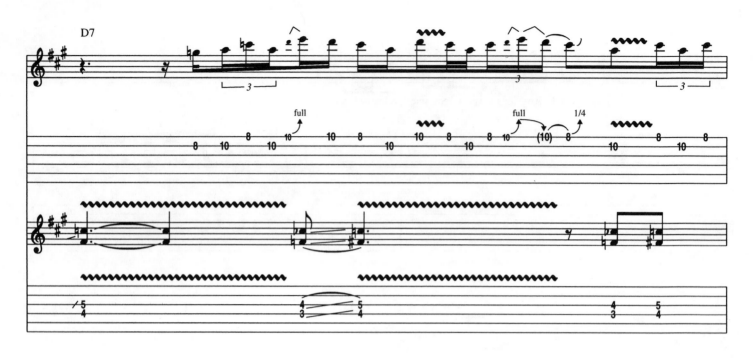

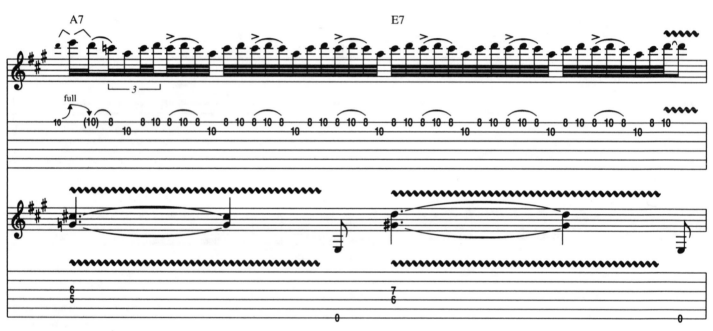

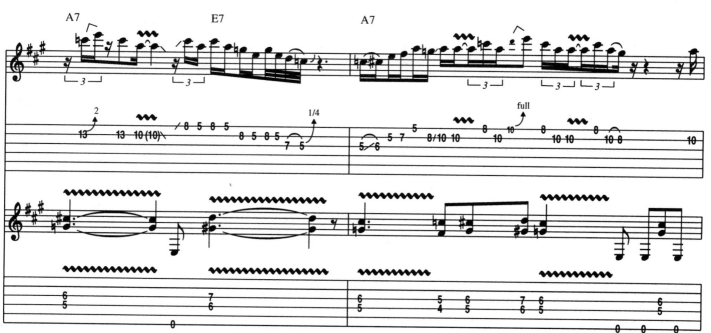

38

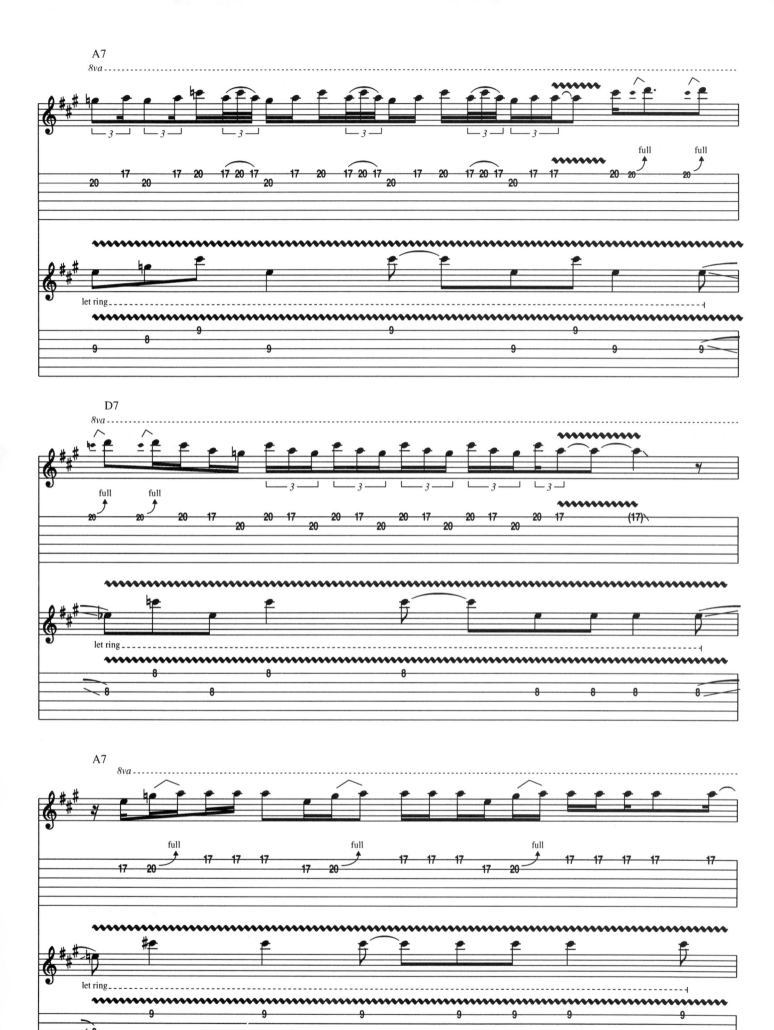

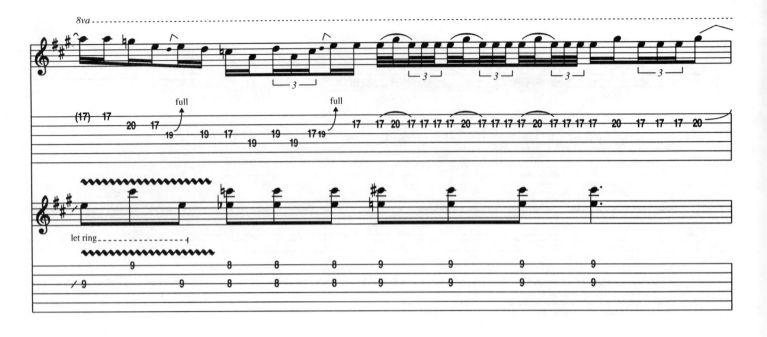

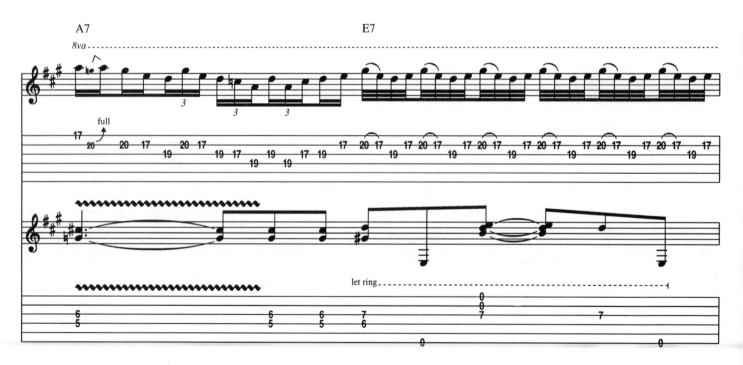

40

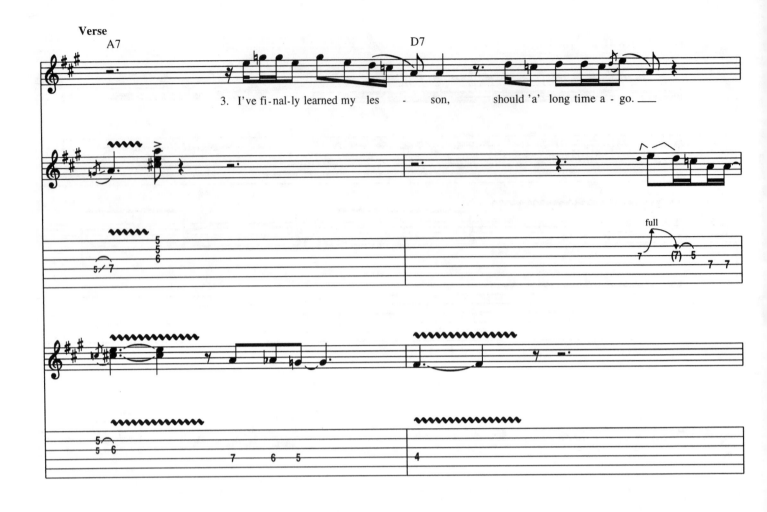

Verse

3. I've fi-nal-ly learned my les - son,   should 'a' long time a - go. ____

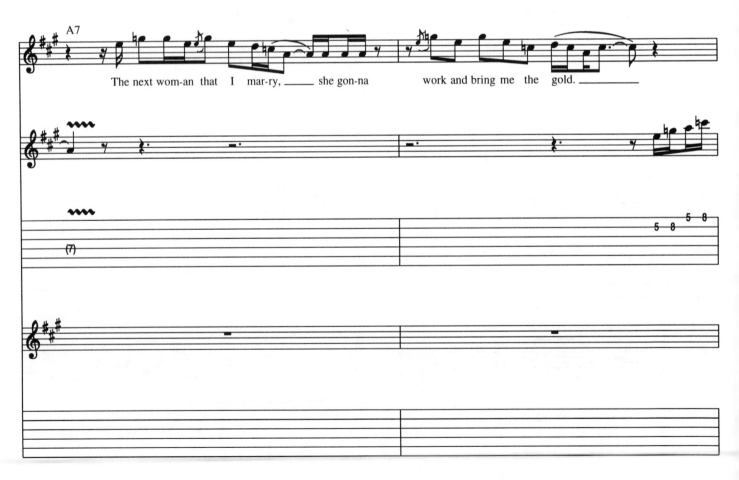

The next wom-an that   I   mar-ry, ____ she gon-na   work and bring me   the   gold. _____

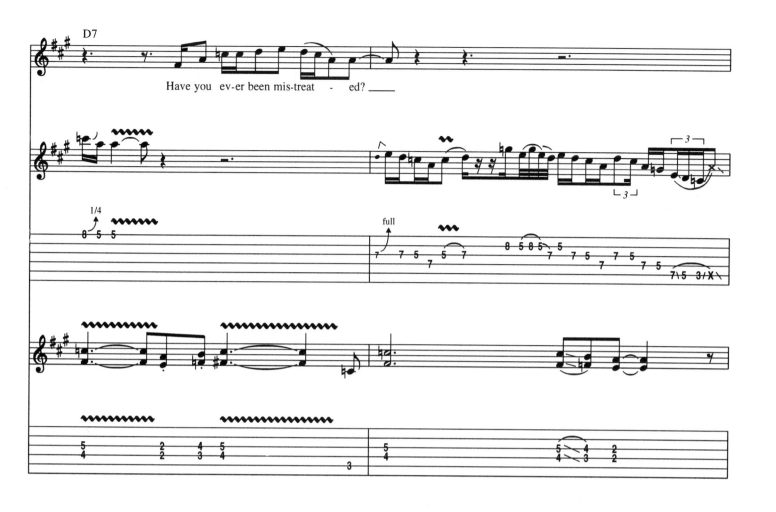

Have you ev-er been mis-treat - ed? _____

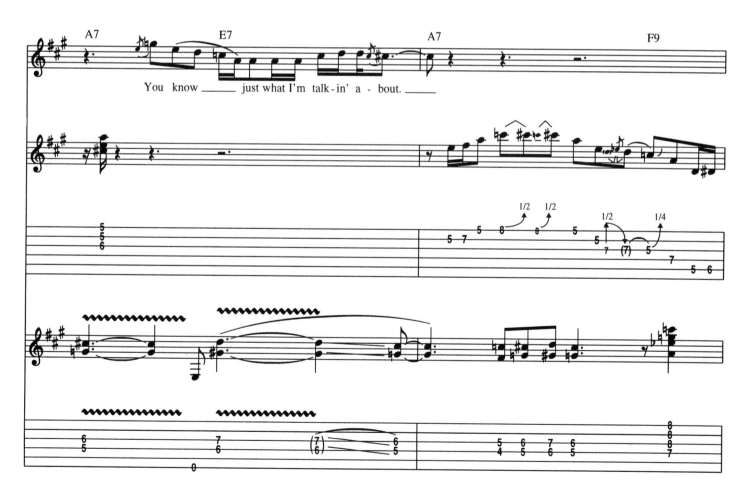

You know _____ just what I'm talk-in' a - bout. _____

It's been five_ long_ years_ for one wom-an,_   she had the nerve,   she had the nerve,   she had the nerve, she had the nerve_

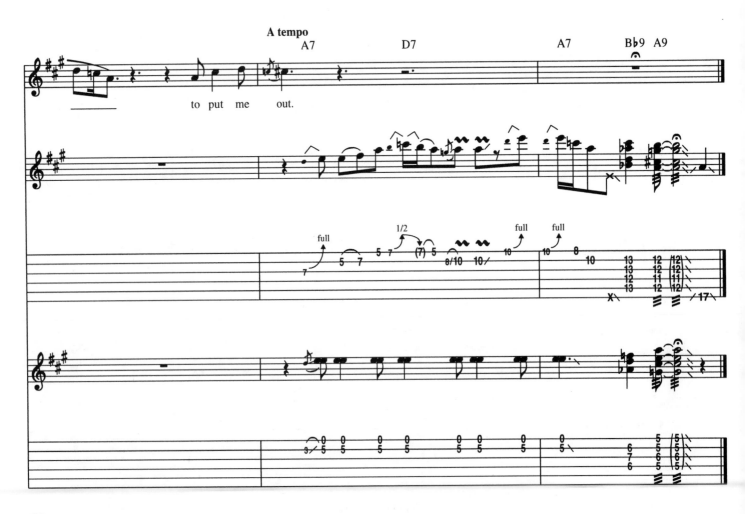

to put me out.

I'm Tore Down

By Sonny Thompson

* Chord symbols reflect suggested tonality.

Chorus

Chorus

Gtr. 2: w/ Rhy. Fig. 1, simile, 1st 7 meas. only

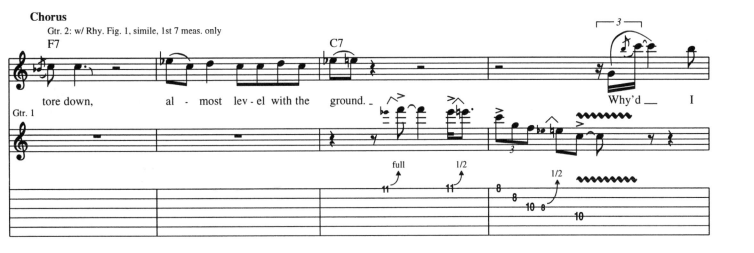

tore down,   al - most lev - el with the   ground. ___   Why'd ___   I

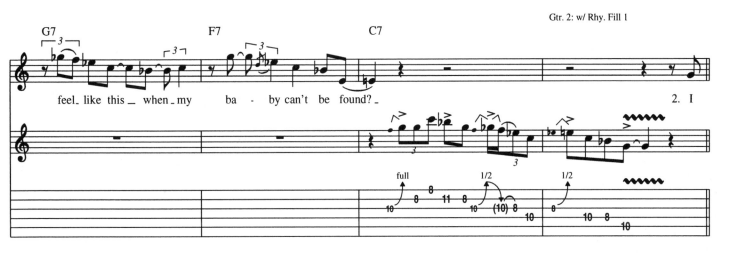

Gtr. 2: w/ Rhy. Fill 1

feel_ like this _ when_ my   ba - by can't be found? _   2. I

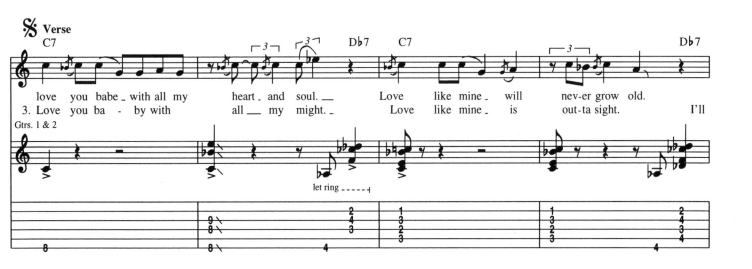

𝄋 Verse

love   you babe _ with all my   heart_ and soul. ___   Love   like mine _ will   nev-er grow old.

3. Love you ba - by with   all ___ my might. _   Love   like mine _ is   out-ta sight.   I'll

Gtrs. 1 & 2

let ring - - - - - ┤

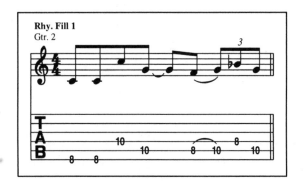

Rhy. Fill 1
Gtr. 2

47

Chorus

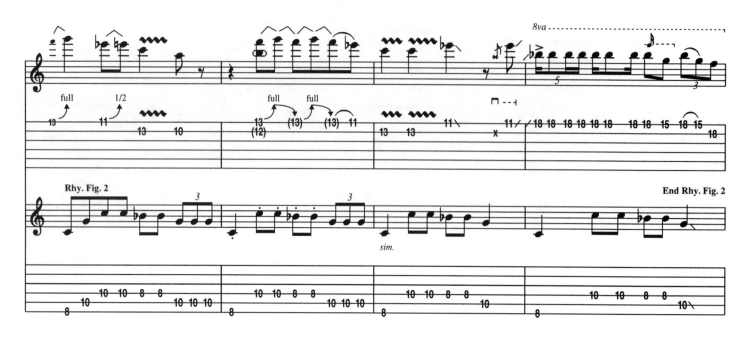

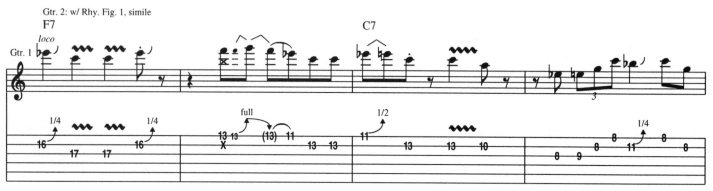

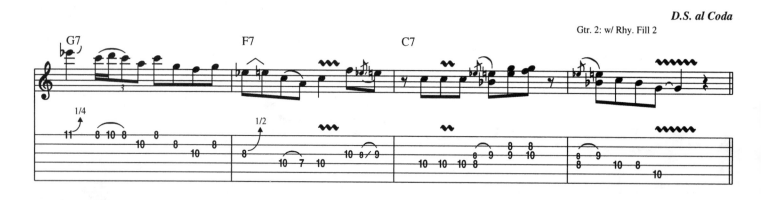

Coda
Chorus

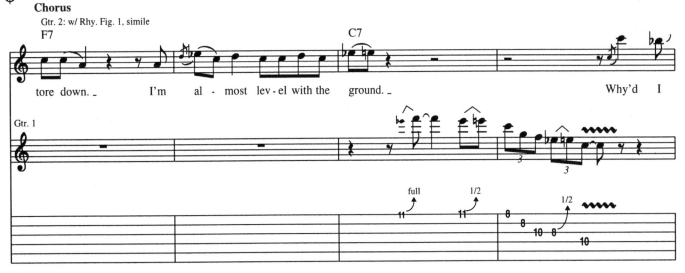

Out-Chorus

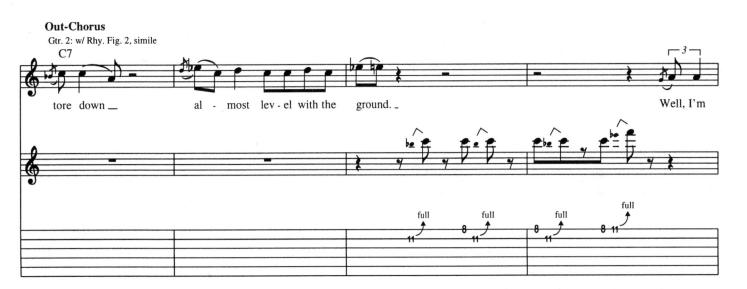

tore down.____ I'm al - most lev-el with the ground.____ Why'd ____ I

feel ____ like this ____ when ____ my ba - by can't be found? ____

Gtr. 1

Gtr. 2

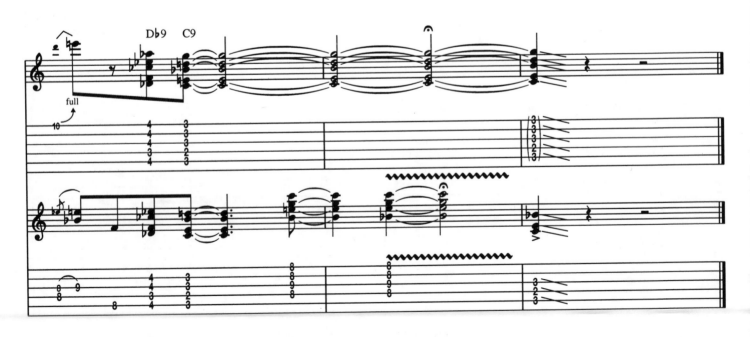

How Long, How Long Blues

Words and Music by Leroy Carr

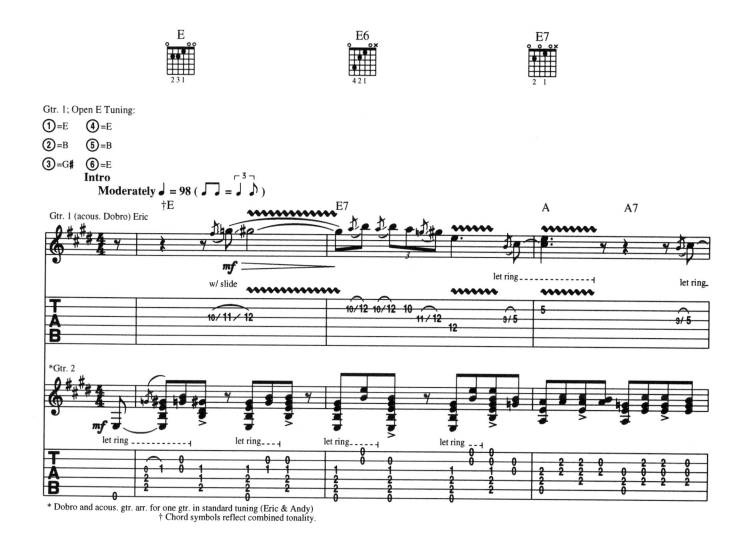

* Dobro and acous. gtr. arr. for one gtr. in standard tuning (Eric & Andy)
† Chord symbols reflect combined tonality.

MCA music publishing

54

Verse
Gtr. 2: w/ Rhy. Fig. 1, 6 7/8 times, simile

2. Went to the sta - tion ___ did-n't see no train. ___ Down in my heart_

___ I have an ach - in' pain. ___ Now, how long, ___ how, how

long, ba - by, how long? 3. I feel dis -

Verse

gust - ed, I feel so bad, __ think-in' 'bout the good time that I once __ had

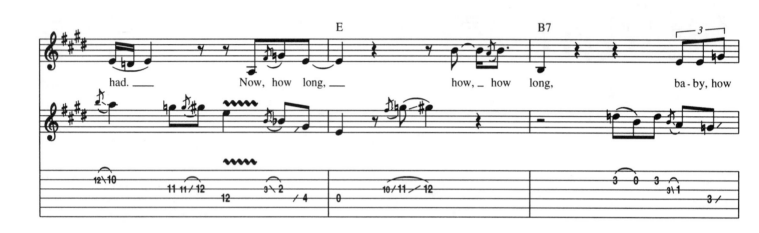

had. __ Now, how long, __ how, __ how long, ba - by, how

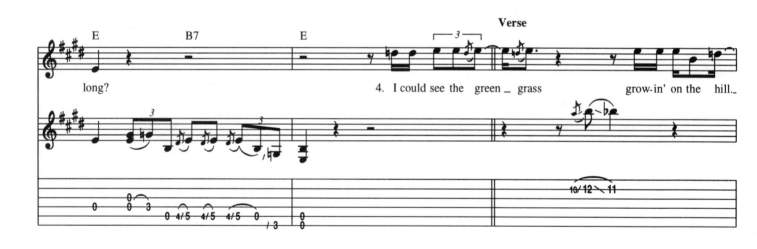

Verse

long? 4. I could see the green __ grass grow-in' on the hill. __

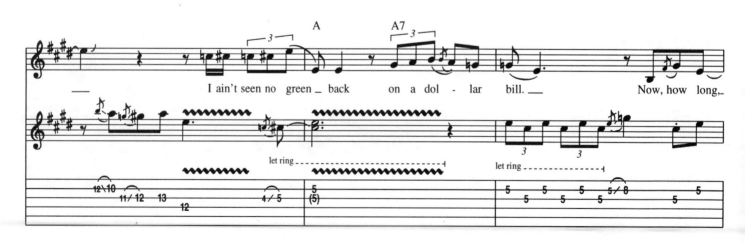

__ I ain't seen no green __ back on a dol - lar bill. __ Now, how long, __

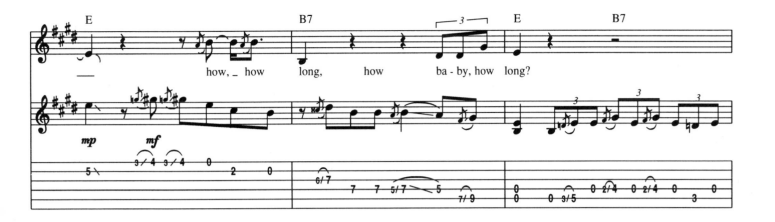

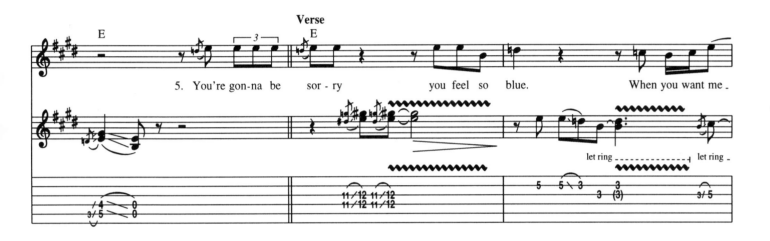

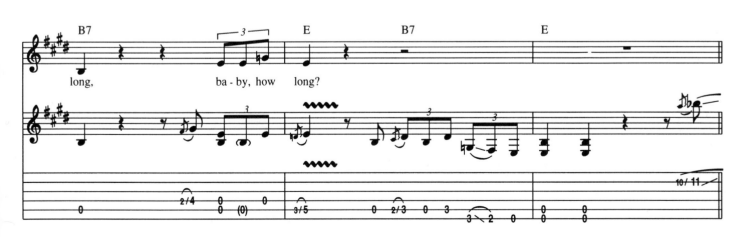

Instrumental Interlude

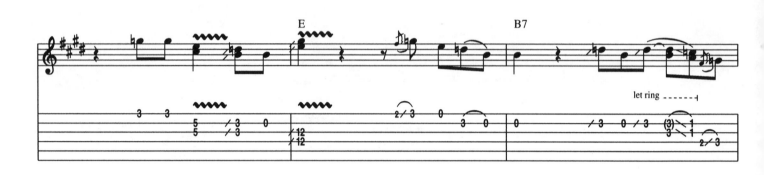

6. Don't have no mon-ey for to ride the

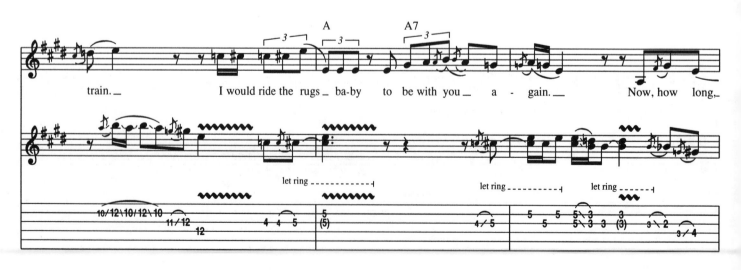

train.___ I would ride the rugs___ ba-by to be with you___ a - gain.___ Now, how long,___

Goin' Away Baby

Written by James A. Lane

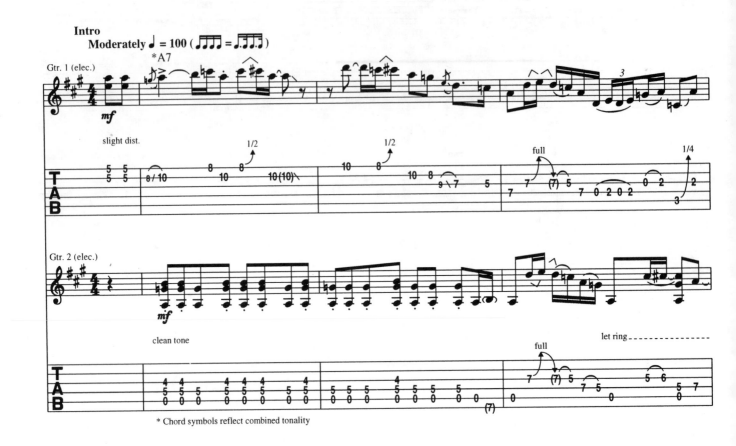

* Chord symbols reflect combined tonality

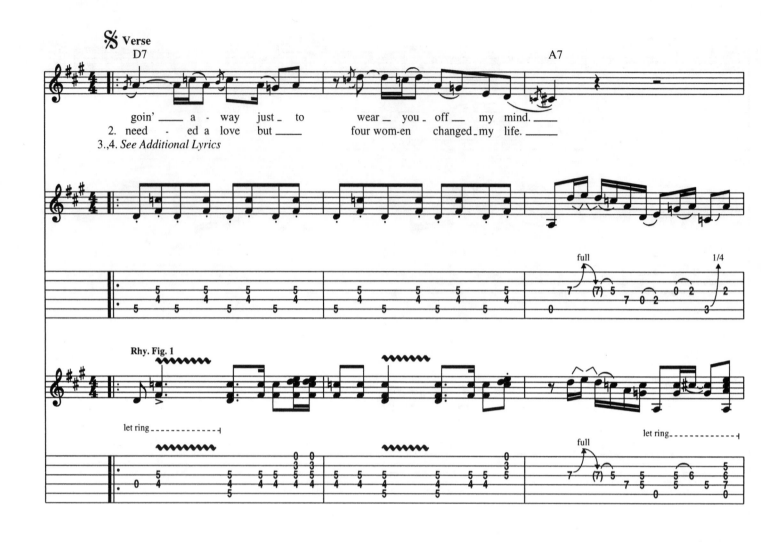

goin' ____ a - way just _ to wear _ you _ off _ my mind. ____
2. need - ed a love but ____ four wom-en changed _ my life. ____
3.,4. *See Additional Lyrics*

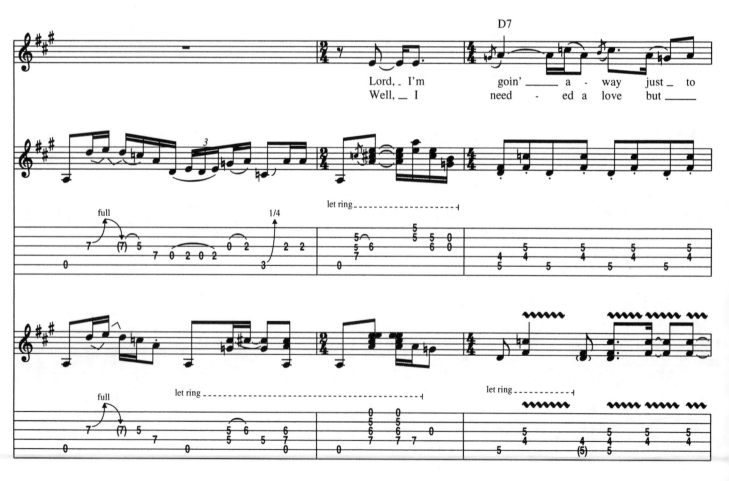

Lord, _ I'm goin' ____ a - way just _ to
Well, _ I need - ed a love but ____

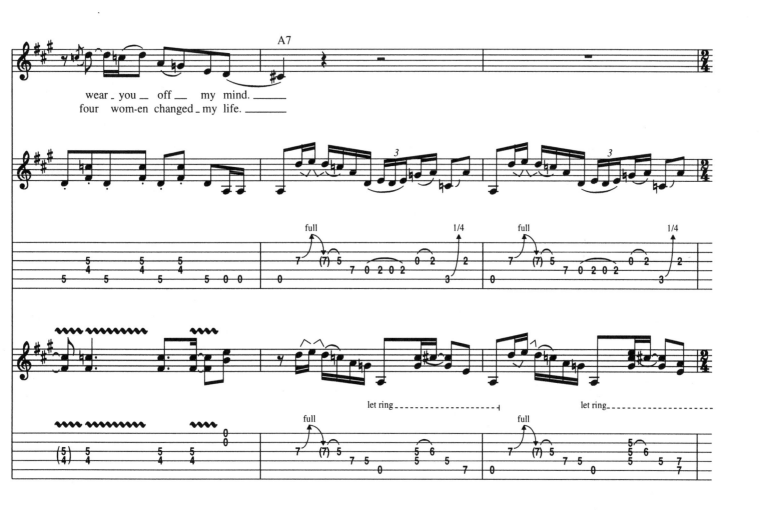

wear _ you _ off _ my mind. _____
four wom-en changed _ my life. _____

Well, _ you _ keep _____ me a wor - ry-in'   'bout it all the _ time. _
Well, _ my _ moth - er and my sis - ter _   treat her and I _ whine. _

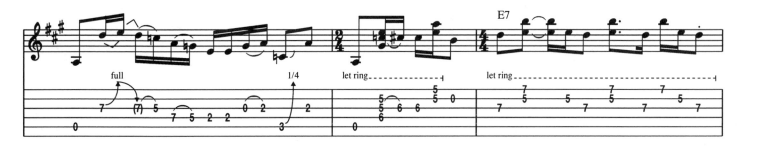

D.S. al Coda

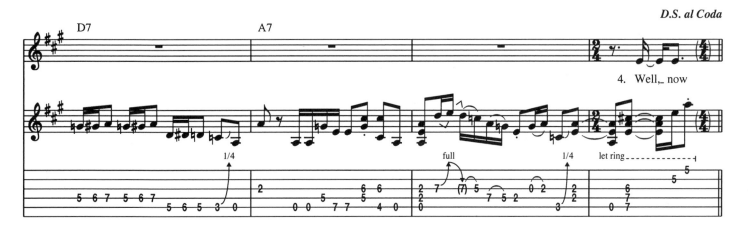

4. Well,_ now

$\oplus$ *Coda*

Gtr. 2: w/ Rhy. Fig. 1, last 3 meas. only

Outro

Gtr. 2: w/ Rhy. Fig. 1, 1st 12 meas. only, simile

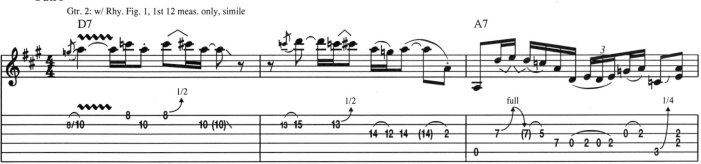

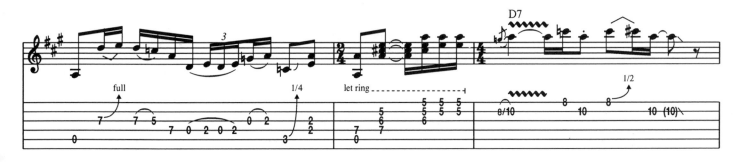

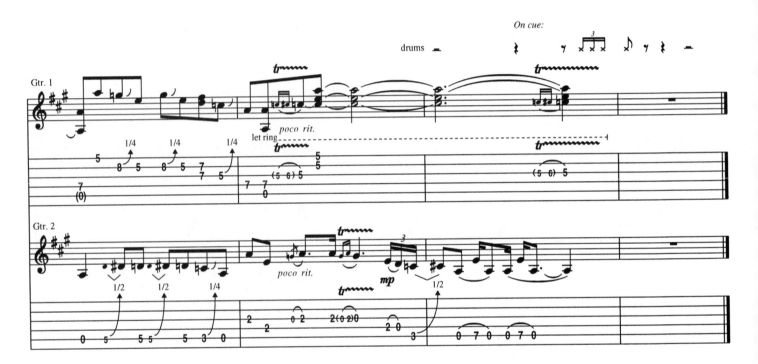

Additional Lyrics

3. If you don't want me, baby,
   Please don't boss me around.
   If you don't want me, baby,
   Please don't boss me around.
   Well, just like you found me,
   You can put me down.

4. Well, now, goodbye baby,
   If you call at home.
   Well, now, goodbye baby,
   If you call at home.
   You can go away,
   Swear you won't stay long.

Blues Leave Me Alone

Written by James A. Lane

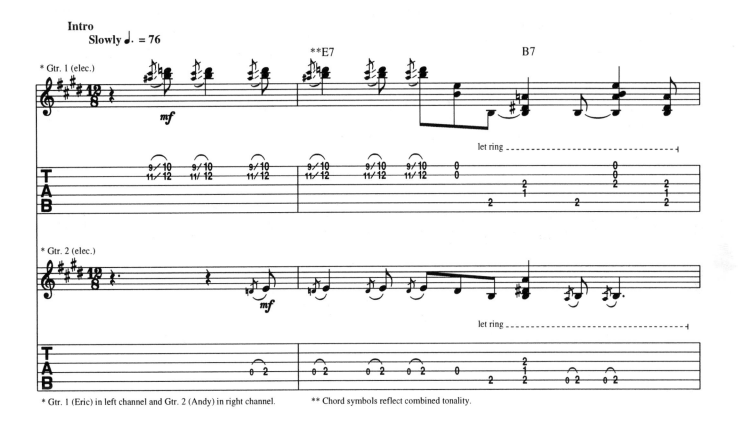

* Gtr. 1 (Eric) in left channel and Gtr. 2 (Andy) in right channel.   ** Chord symbols reflect combined tonality.

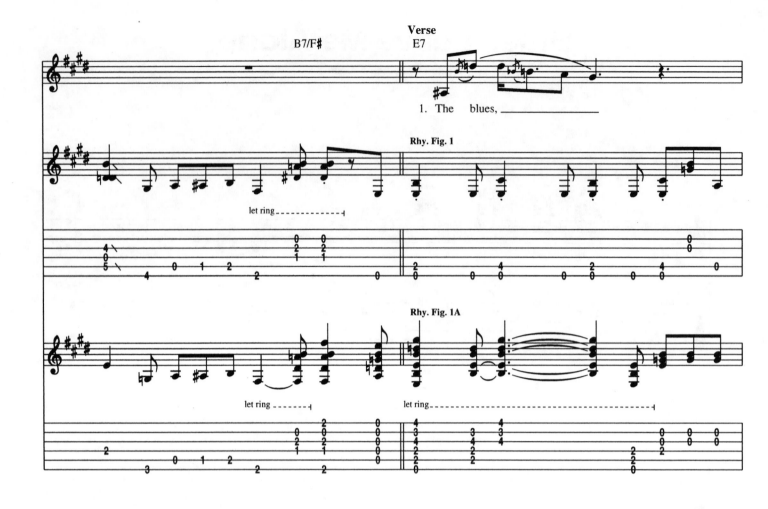

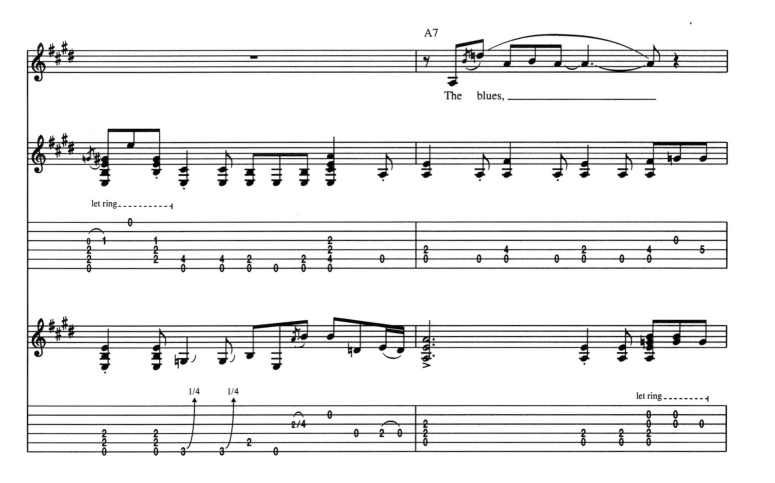

The blues, _____

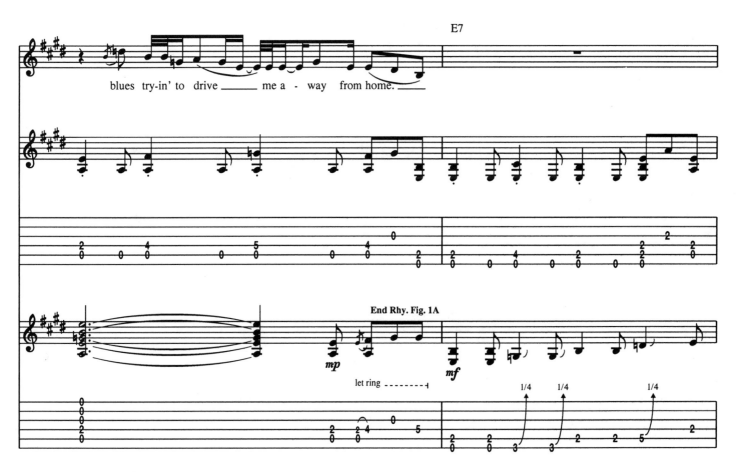

blues try-in' to drive ____ me a - way from home. ____

End Rhy. Fig. 1A

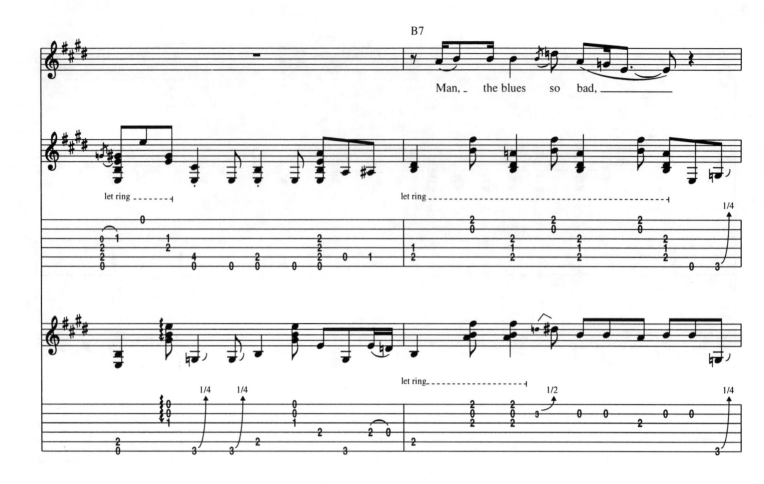

Man,_ the blues so bad,_____

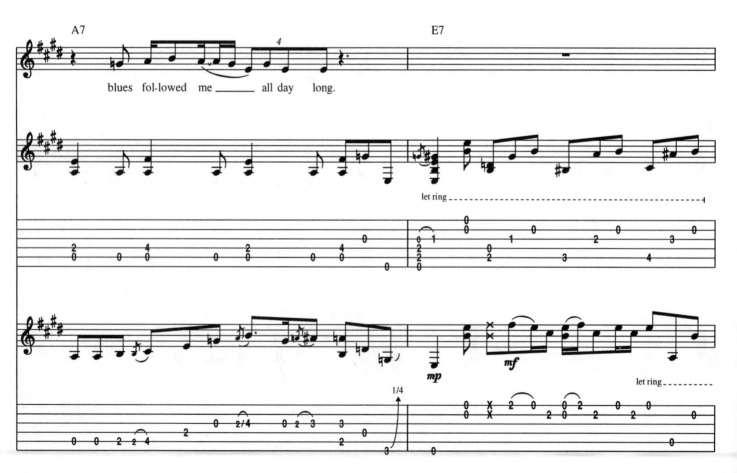

blues fol-lowed me _____ all day long.

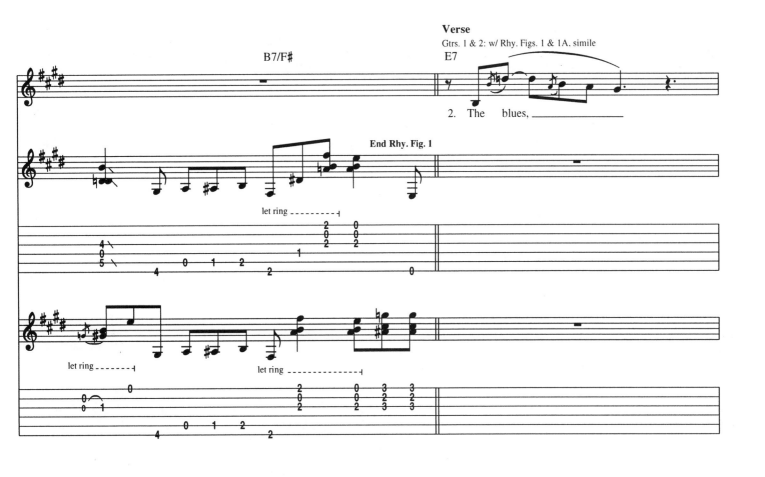

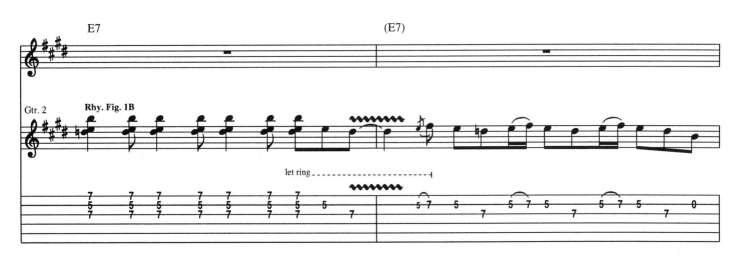

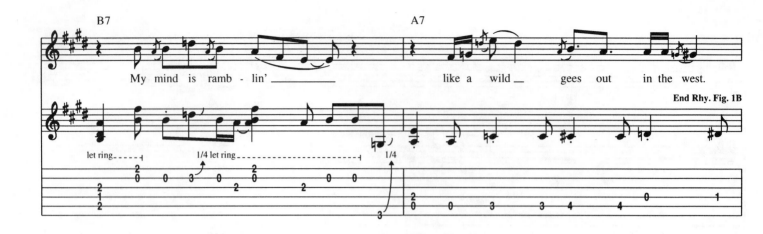

My mind is ramb - lin' _____ like a wild _ gees out in the west.

End Rhy. Fig. 1B

3. Well, in my all _

Verse

Gtrs. 1 & 2: w/ Rhy. Figs. 1 & 1A, simile

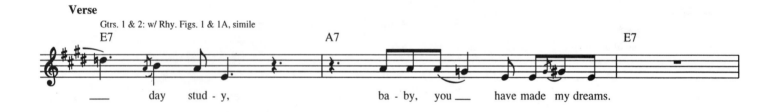

_ day stud - y, ba - by, you _ have made my dreams.

Yes, in my all _ day stud - y ba - by, you _ my mid-night dream._

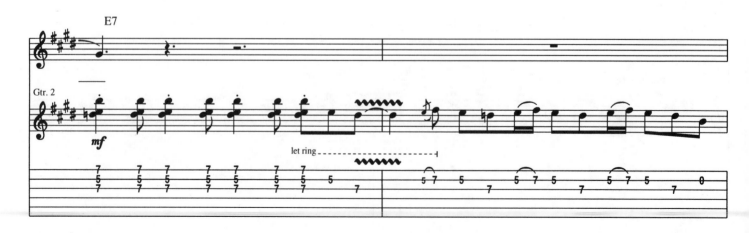

Gtr. 2

72

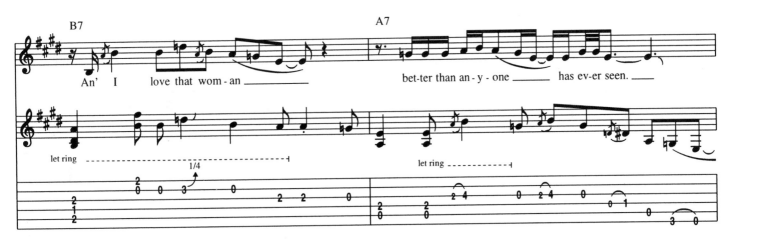

An' I love that wom - an _____ bet-ter than an - y - one _____ has ev-er seen.

Harmonica Solo

Gtr. 1: w/ Rhy. Fig. 1, 1st 4 meas. only, simile

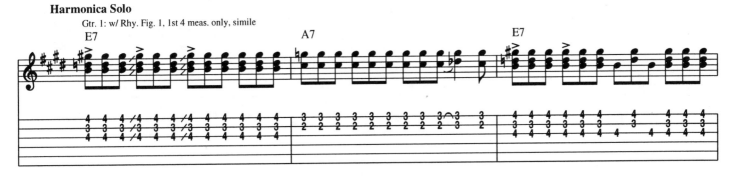

Verse

Gtr. 1: w/ Rhy. Fig. 1, 1st 10 meas. only, simile
Gtr. 2: w/ Rhy. Fig. 1A

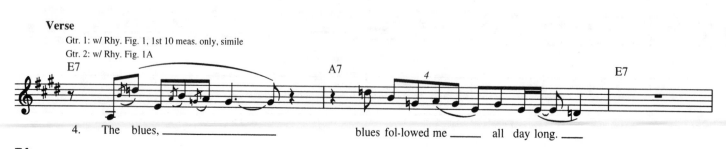

4. The blues, _____ blues fol-lowed me ____ all day long. ____

The blues, _____ blues fol-lowed me _____ all day long. _____

Gtr. 2: w/ Rhy. Fig. 1B

Blues,___ blues, blues,_____

blues won't you please _ leave me a-lone.

Sinner's Prayer

Words and Music by Lloyd C. Glenn and Lowell Fulson

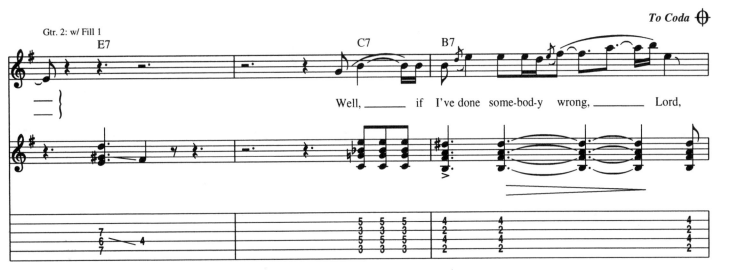

Gtr. 2: w/ Fill 1

Well, _____ if I've done some-bod-y wrong, _____ Lord,

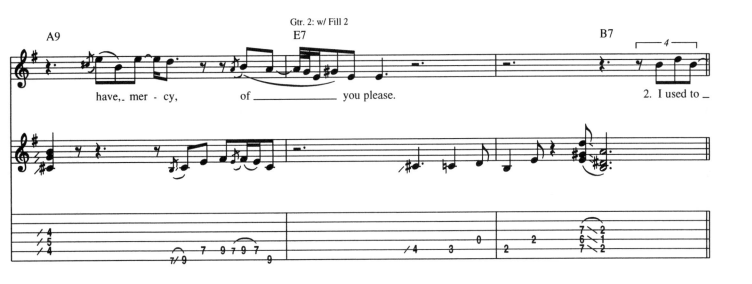

Gtr. 2: w/ Fill 2

have, mer - cy, of _____ you please.

2. I used to

Rhy. Fill 2
Gtr. 1

mf

Fill 1
*Gtr. 2(dist.)

mf

let ring   let ring

*Eric

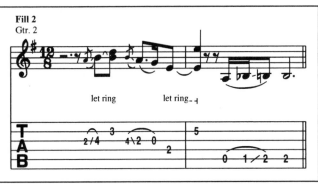

Fill 2
Gtr. 2

let ring   let ring

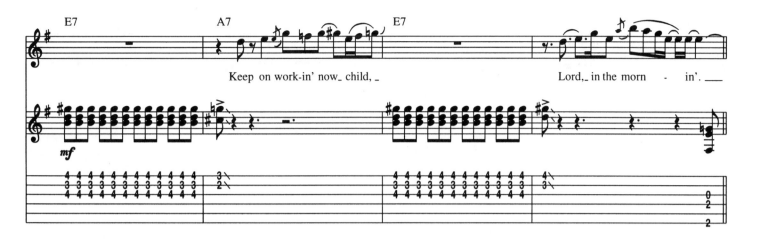

Keep on work-in' now child, Lord, in the morn - in'.

Guitar Solo

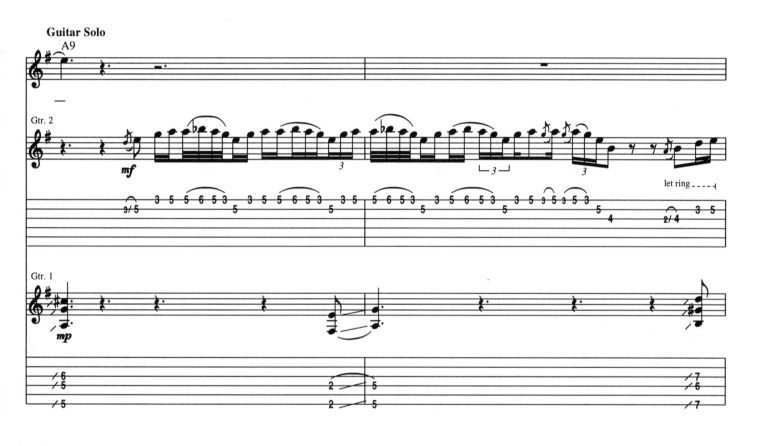

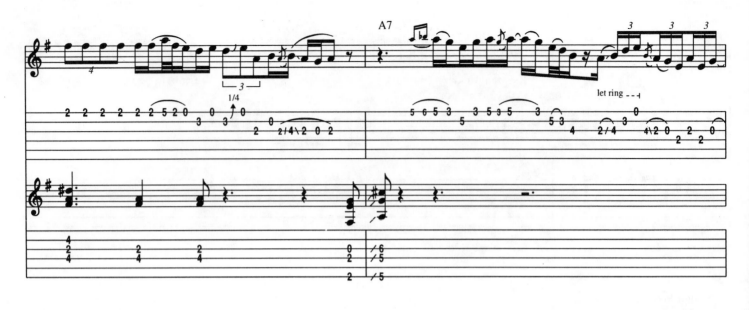

D.S. al Coda

3. Well, ___ if

✛ *Coda*

have ___ mer - cy, ___ if you please. ___ Whoa, ho, ho, ___ Lord.

Motherless Child

Words and Music by Eric Clapton and Carl Radle

Gtrs. 1 & 2: Open G Tuning, Capo IV

① = D   ④ = D
② = B   ⑤ = G
③ = G   ⑥ = D

Gtr. 3: Standard Tuning

Intro

Moderately Fast ♩ = 156

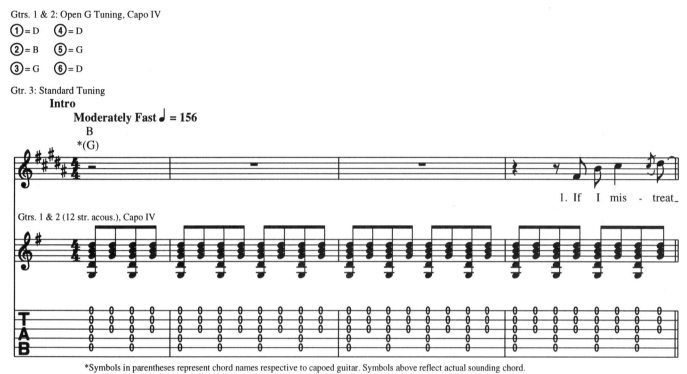

*Symbols in parentheses represent chord names respective to capoed guitar. Symbols above reflect actual sounding chord.

Verse

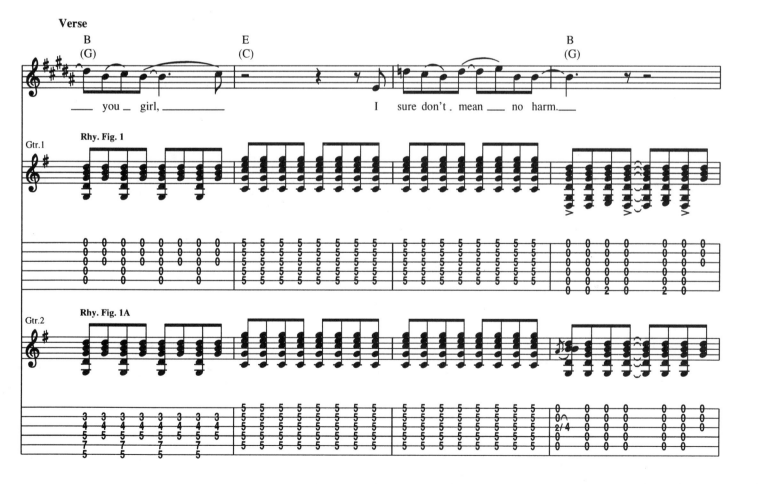

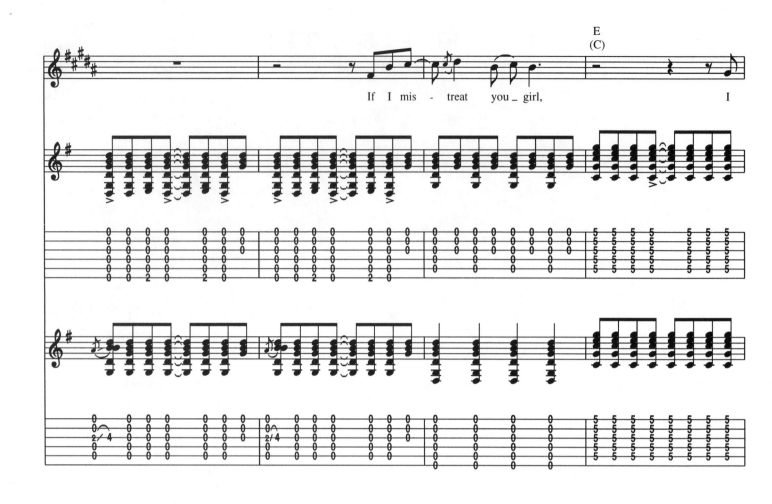

If I mis - treat you _ girl,   I

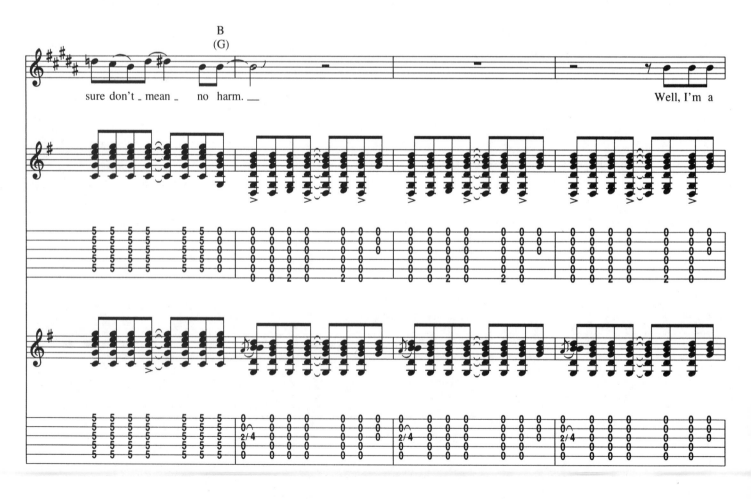

sure don't _ mean _ no harm. _   Well, I'm a

84

Hell, I did more for you girl, _____ than _ your dad-dy ev - er done. _

Well, I give you my jew - el - ry _

1.,2.
*
an' he ain't give _____ you _ none.

*extra measure of F♯7

5. An' when you

3.
B
(G)
_____ here.

5. An' when you

Gtr. 3: w/ Rhy. Fill 1

Gtr. 1

Gtr. 2

Gtr. 3

Additional Lyrics

5. An' when you see two women,
   Always runnin' hand in hand,
   And when you see two women,
   Always runnin' hand in hand,
   You can bet your bottom dollar,
   One got the other one's man.

6. But I'm goin' to the river,
   Get me a tangled rockin' chair.
   I'm goin' to the river
   Get me a tangled rockin' chair.
   And if the blues over take me,
   Take me away from here.

It Hurts Me Too

By Mel London

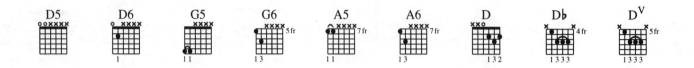

Gtr. 1: Open D Tuning,   Gtr. 2: "Drop D" Tuning,
Down 1/2 Step: Down 1/2 Step:

①＝Db ④＝Db   ①＝Eb ④＝Db

②＝Ab ⑤＝Ab   ②＝Bb ⑤＝Ab

③＝F   ⑥＝Db   ③＝Gb ⑥＝Db

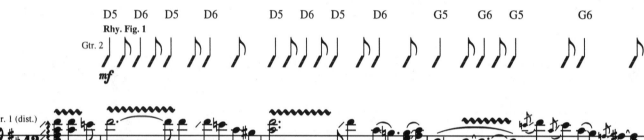

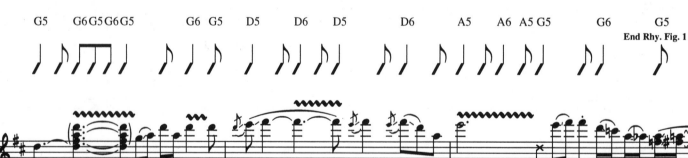

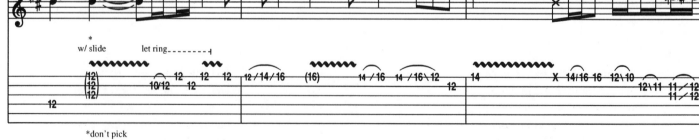

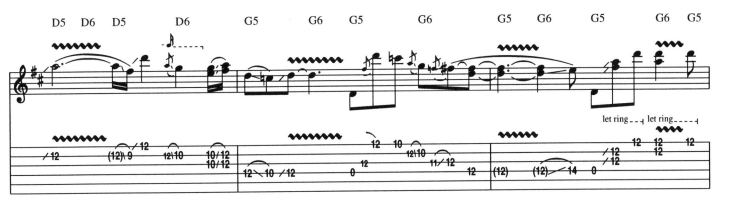

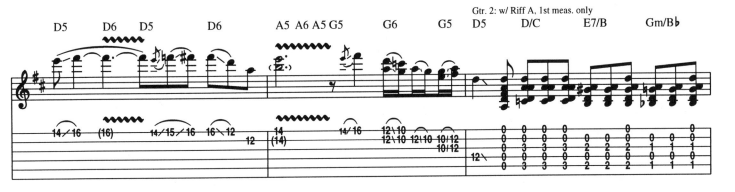

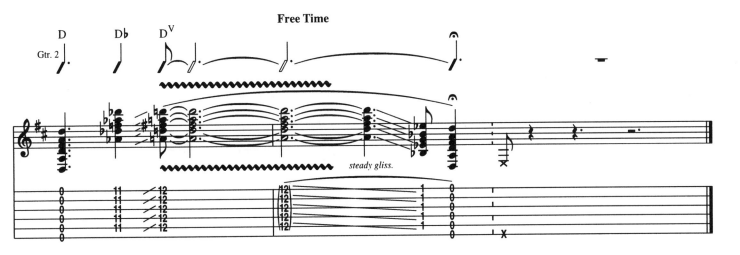

Additional Lyrics

3. He'll love another woman,
   An' I love you.
   Lord, you love him,
   An' stick to him like glue.
   When things go wrong,
   Go wrong with you,
   It hurts me too.

4. Now, you better leave him,
   He better put you down.
   Lord, I won't stand to see you
   Pushed around.
   When things go wrong,
   Go wrong with you,
   It hurts me too.

Someday After A While (You'll Be Sorry)

By Freddie King and Sonny Thompson

Verse

1. I ___ got ___ to ride ___ that lone - some train. ___ My ___ heart is heav - y ___ with

Rhy. Fig. 1

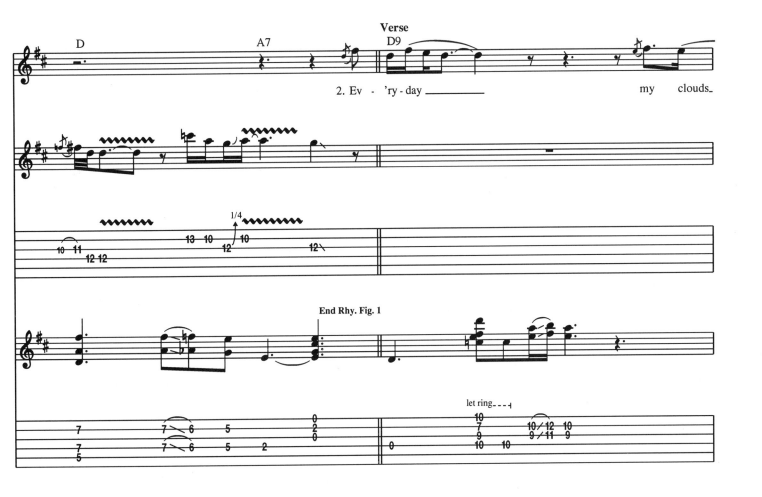

Verse
2. Ev - 'ry-day _____ my clouds _____

End Rhy. Fig. 1

_____ are grey, _____ takes you to roll _____ all

_ down the line. _

E7

I don't need, _ I don't need no _

hold bend   hold bend

full   full

let ring - - - - - - -

let ring - - - - - - - - - - -

sym-pa-thy,   so babe,   babe, _   don't you, _

A

Outro Solo

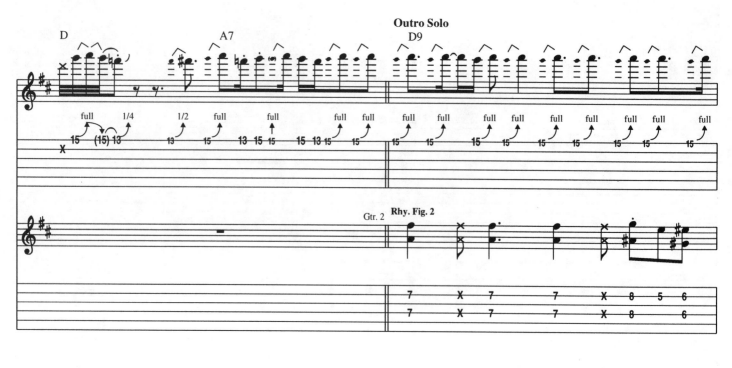

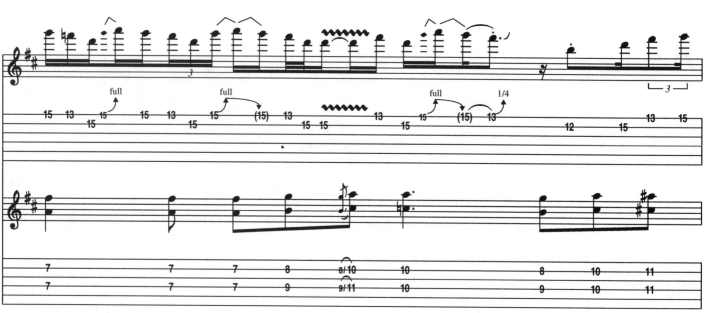

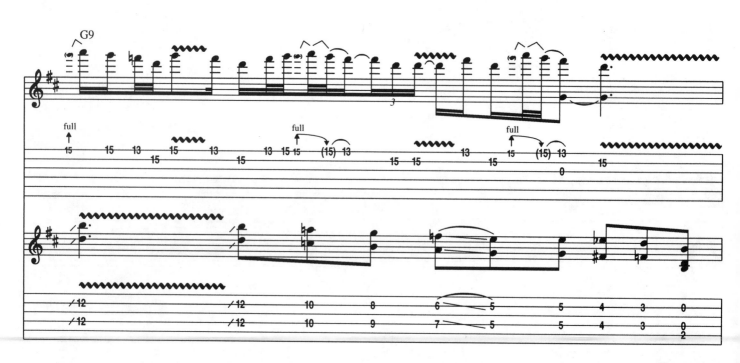

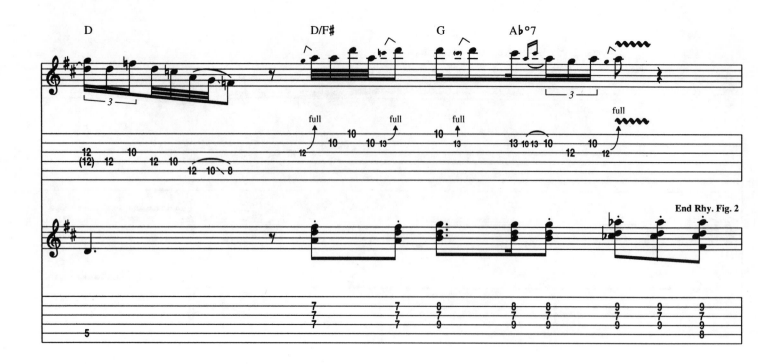

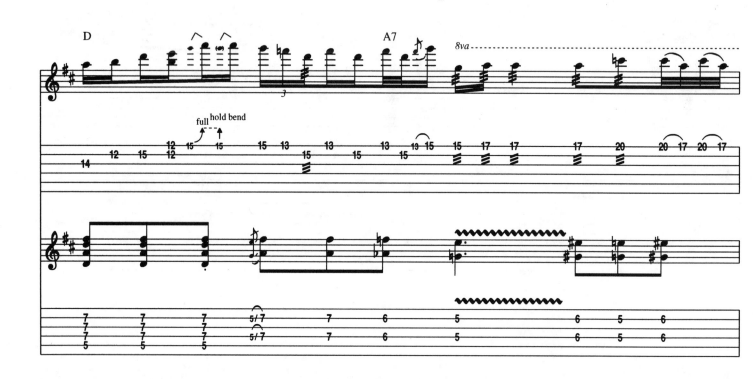

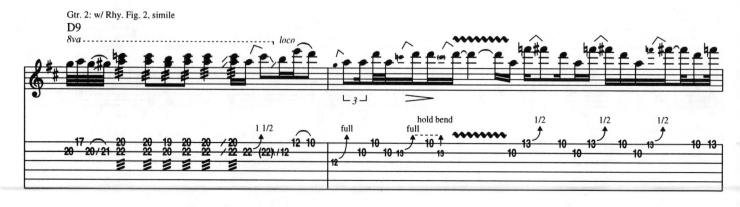

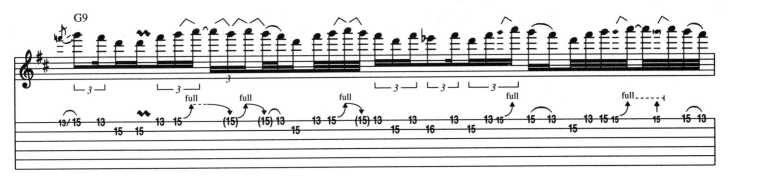

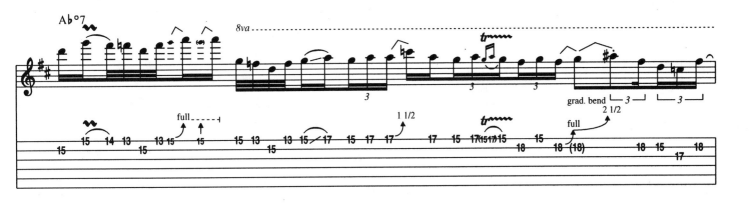

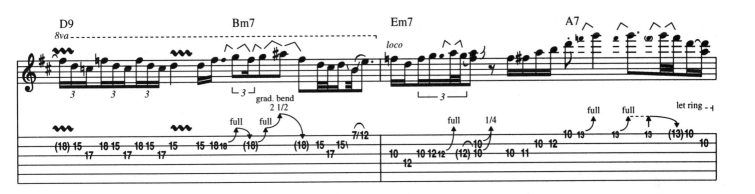

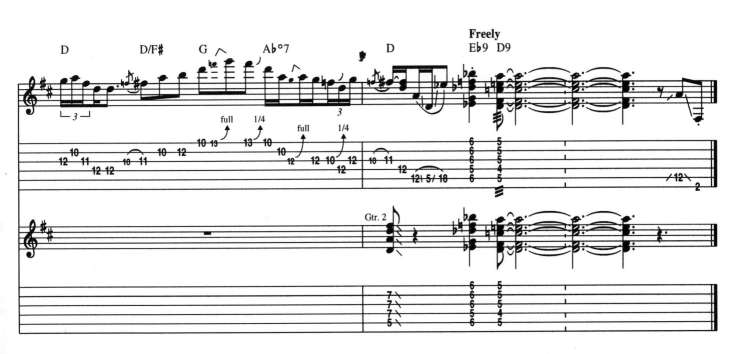

Standin' Around Crying

Written by Muddy Waters

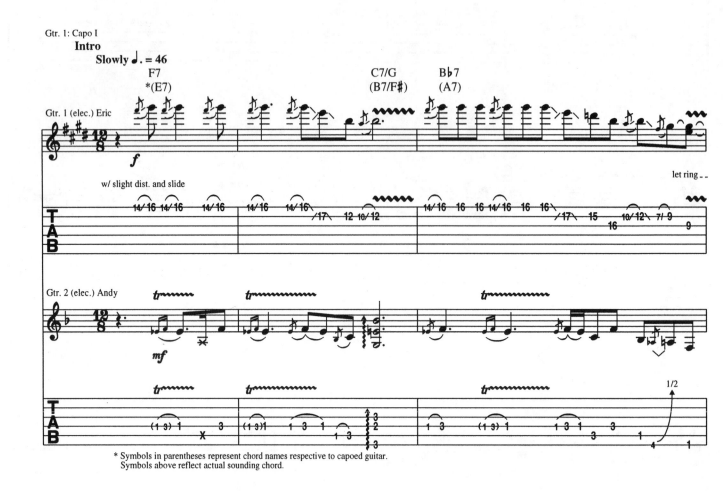

* Symbols in parentheses represent chord names respective to capoed guitar.
Symbols above reflect actual sounding chord.

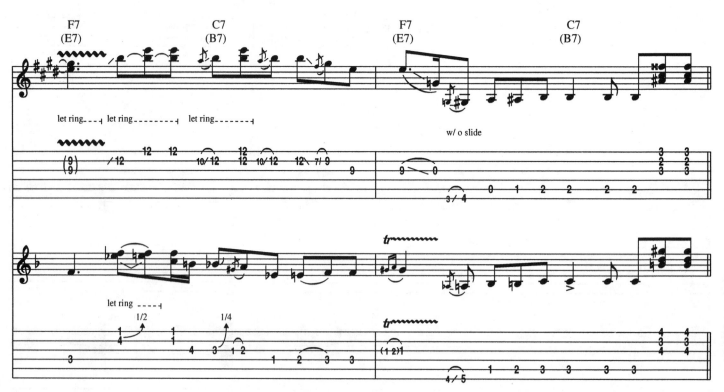

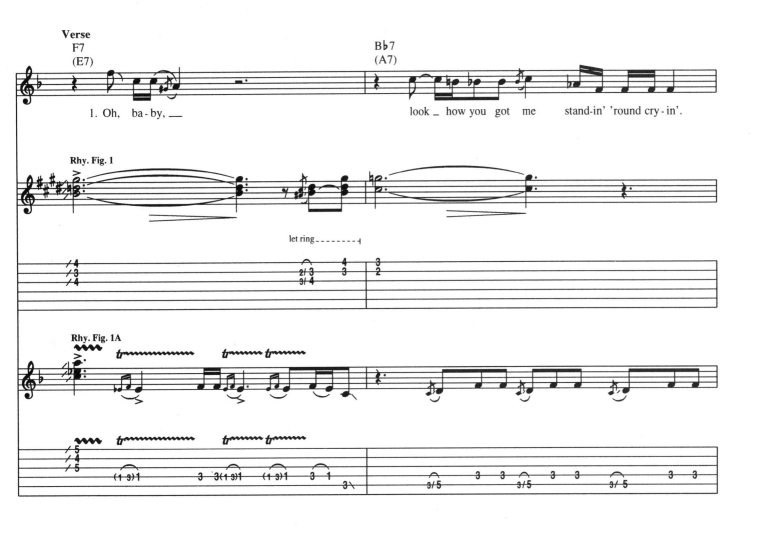

Verse

1. Oh, ba-by, ___ look ___ how you got me stand-in' 'round cry-in'.

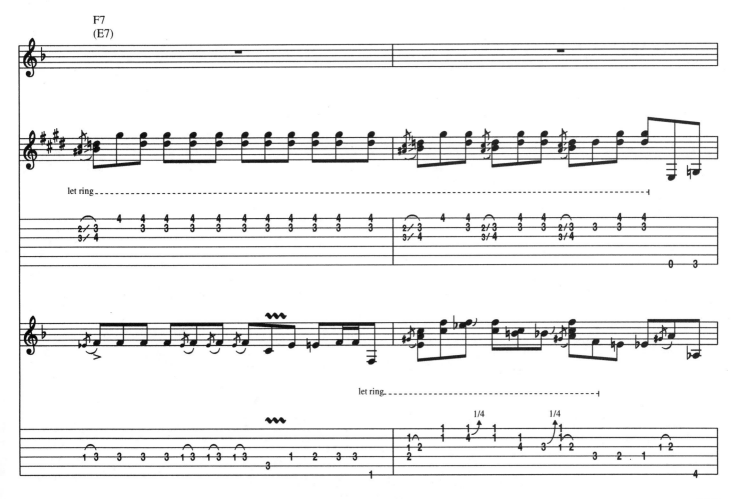

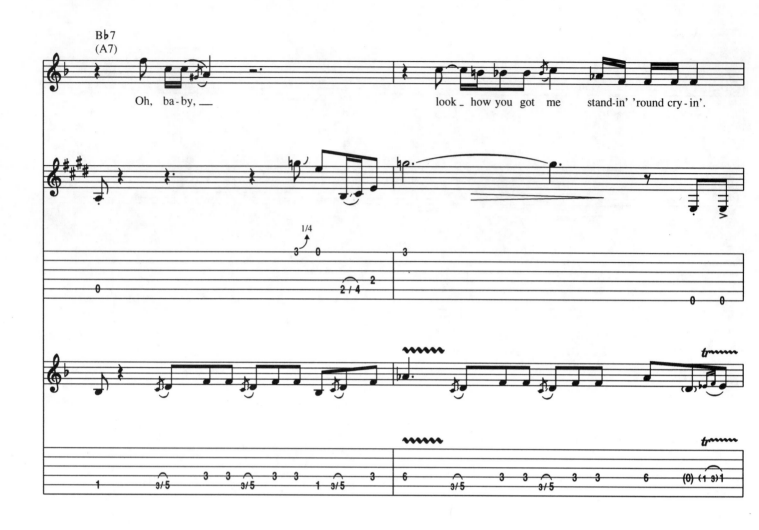

Oh, ba - by, __ look _ how you got me stand-in' 'round cry - in'.

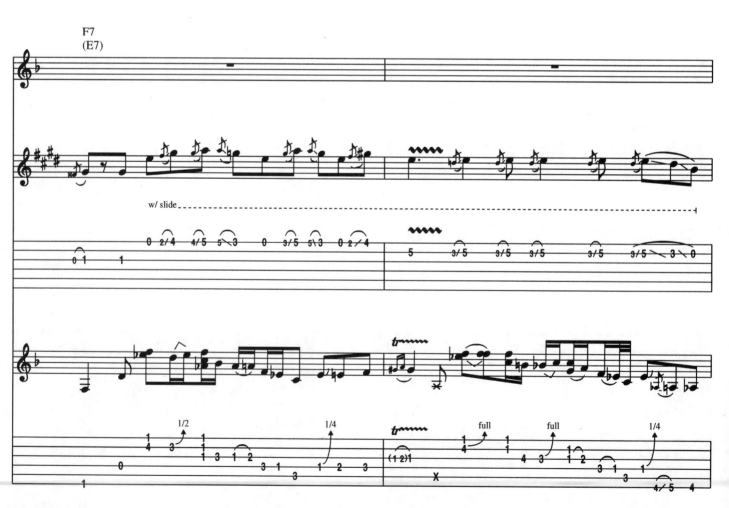

No, I don't love you lit-tle girl,   but you're al-ways   rest - in' on my mind.

Driftin'

Words and Music by Charles Brown, Johnny Moore and Eddie Williams

* Chord symbols represent suggested harmony.

if my ba - by ____ would on - ly take me back ____ a-gain,

I would feel ____ much bet - ter dar - lin',

an' at least I'd have ____ a friend.

Guitar Solo

Verse

Gtr. 1: w/ Rhy. Fig. 1, simile

3. I give you all my mon - ey, tell me what more can I do? __

An' give y'all my mon - ey,

tell me what more can __ I do? __

You was a sweet lit - tle girl, _____ but I swear you won't _____ be true. __

D.S. al Coda

4. An' I'm drift - in' an' drift - in', ____

Coda

me.

Outro

111

Groaning The Blues

Written by Willie Dixon

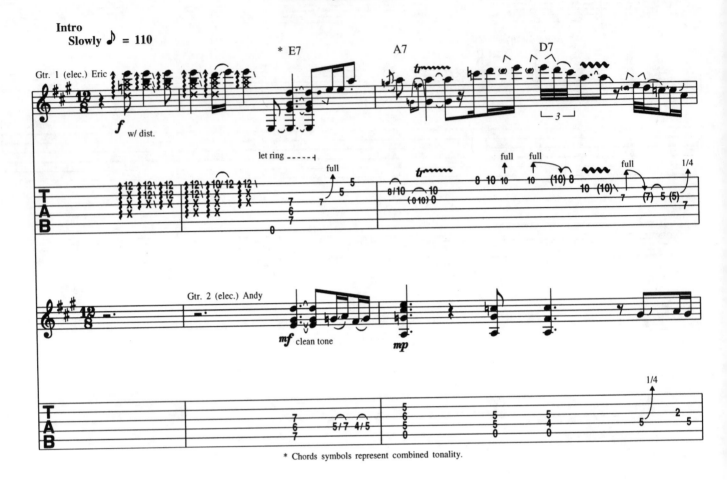

* Chords symbols represent combined tonality.

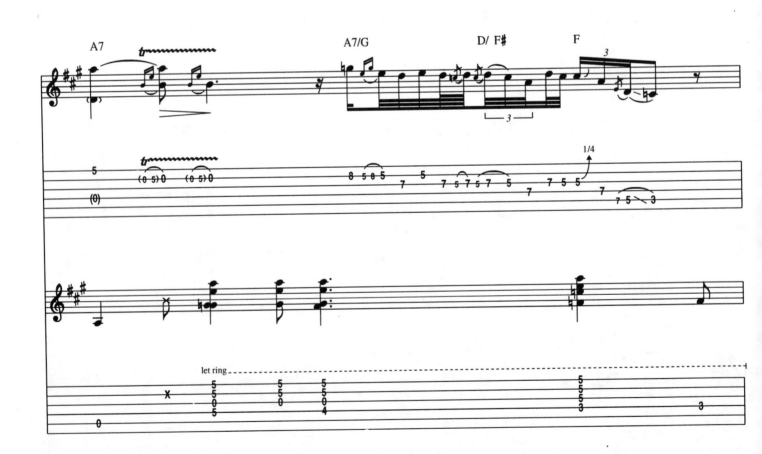

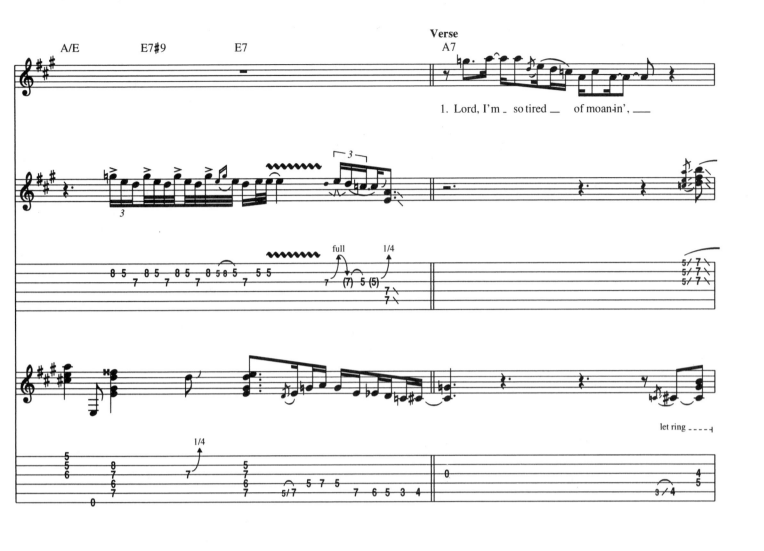

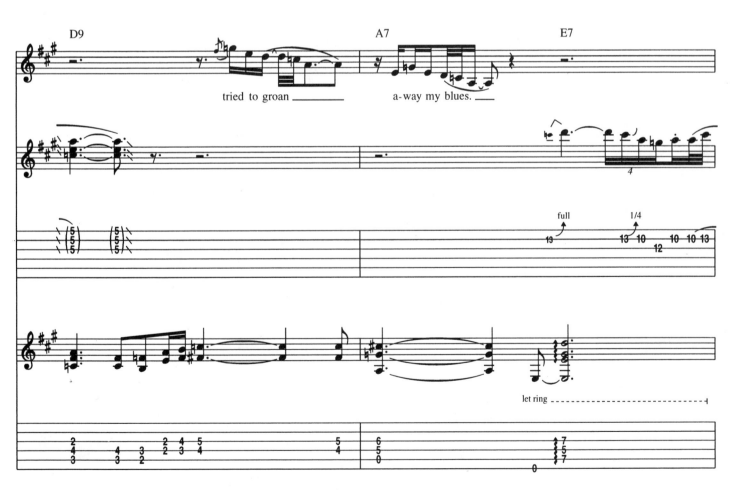

I'm _ so tired _ of moan-in', _

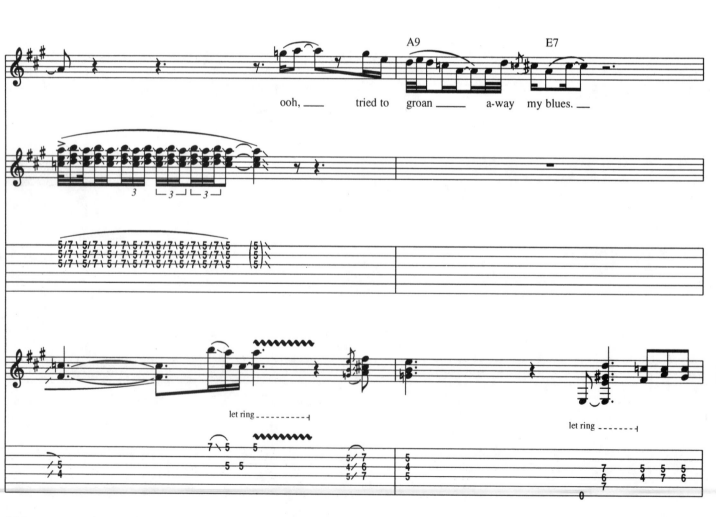

ooh, _____ tried to groan _____ a-way my blues. _____

let ring - - - - - - - - -|

let ring - - - - - -|

114

2. I would rath-er die _____ of _ star-va-tion _

than be shot _ in the de-sert sun.

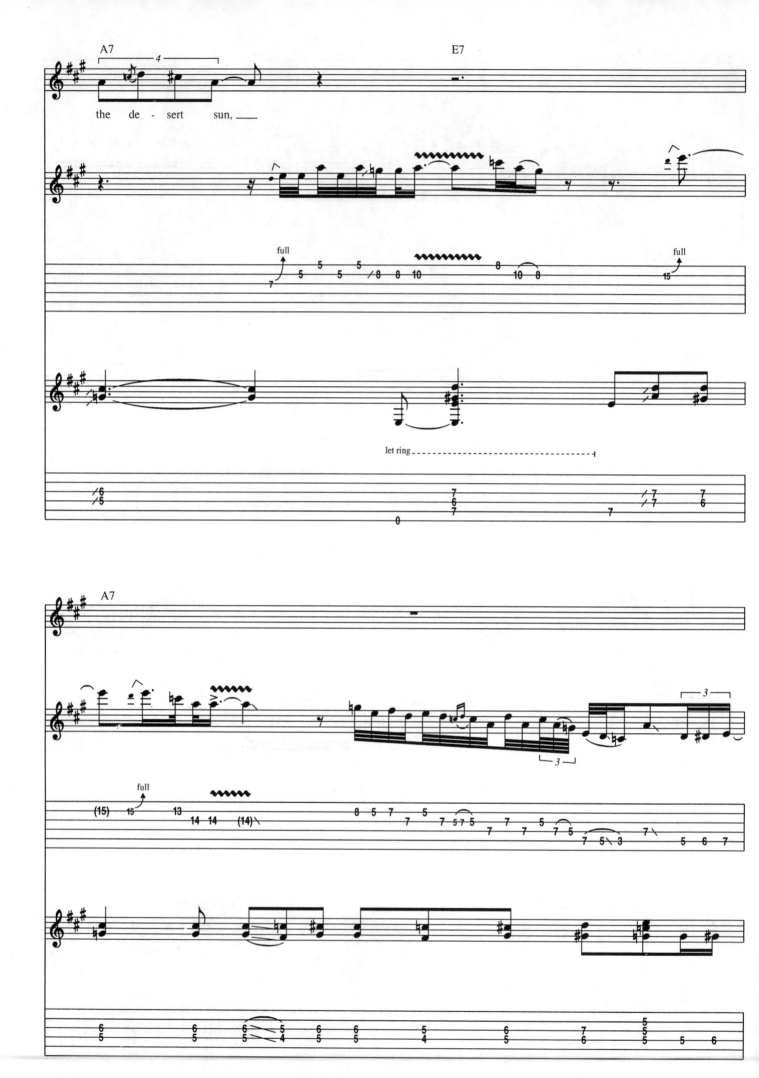

Guitar Solo

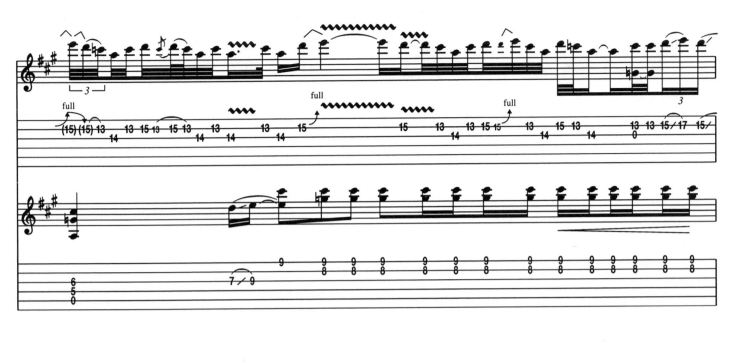

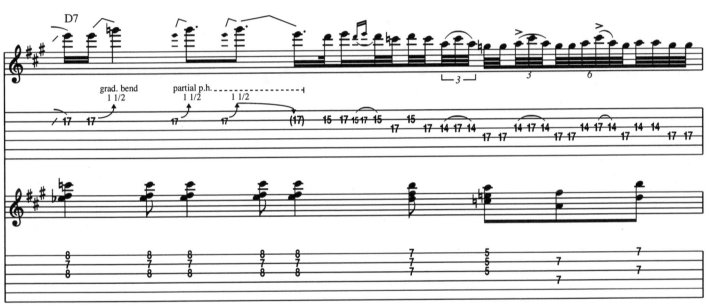

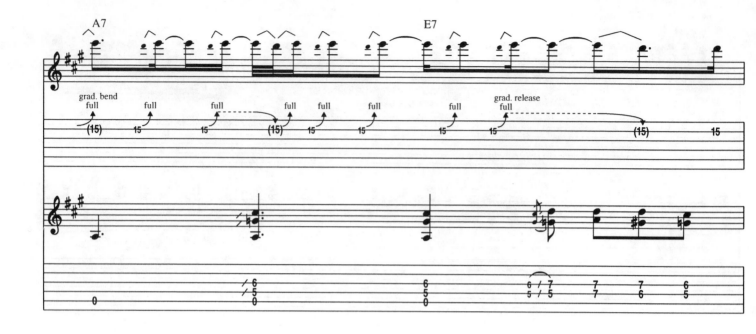

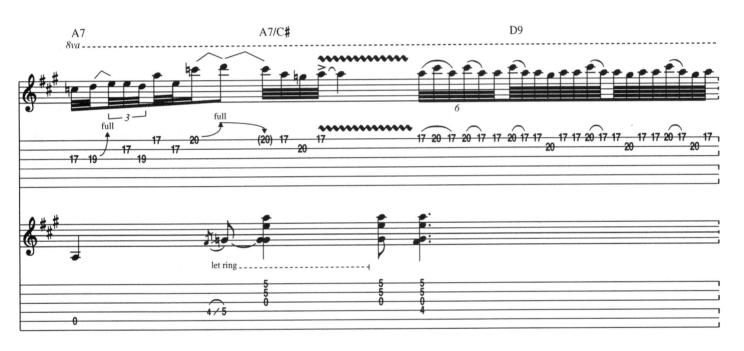

Verse
3. My whole heart ___ gets so heav-y ___

Lord, I ___ shakes ___ down in my bones.

My heart ___ gets so heav-y ___

124

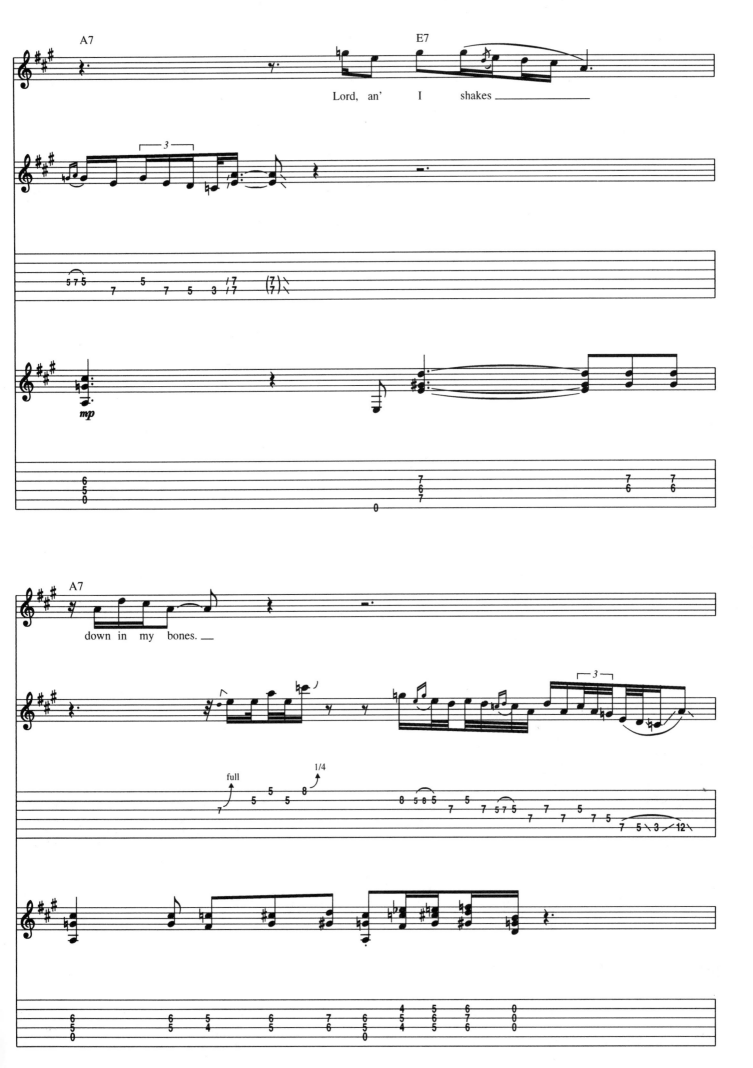

Lord, an' I shakes _____

down in my bones. __

I can't hol-ler mur-der, ___ ooh, ___ Lord, but I'm for _____ to weep and moan. ___

126

NOTATION LEGEND